NITE

Never Invite The Enemy

Ellen Grant

ISBN 978-1-63874-240-1 (paperback)
ISBN 978-1-63874-241-8 (digital)

Christian Faith Publishing, Inc.
832 Park Avenue
Meadville, PA 16335
www.christianfaithpublishing.com

Printed in the United States of America

This book is dedicated to
My husband, Nathan Prevalent Brooks
My parents, Rev. Linton Grant* and family
phenomenal matriarch, Glendora Grant
My siblings, Gogi Laurent, Karen* and Terry
Franklin*, Eric and Charlene Grant
My trailblazers nieces Molly (Terri) Franklin,
Lauren Laurent and Jade Grant
My adorable nieces Erica, Nika and nephews, Grant, Daniel, EJ
Aunt, Helen "Nanny" Wilfred
Sister/cousin, Priscilla Ann Joseph
Thanks again for your steadfast love, encouragement and
patience as we, never me, embark on this journey again.

*In memory

Contents

Introduction

Mason and Chloe met in their collegiate years. They dated for two years before the relationship ended, given Mason's noncommittal mindset. Chloe was thinking forever while Mason indulged in here and now. He flaunted his six-foot-three physique he inherited from his father. Mason—tall, dark, and handsome—was the obvious cookie cutter. To his advantage, some women willingly navigated to the flirtatious eye candy.

Women, partying, and good times were Mason and his friends', Rick, Jeff, Alfonzo, and Dris, main objective. The rat pack were teammates, fraternity brothers, as well as best friends. After graduating, four among the friends worked for corporations. Jeff lives on the west coast. Alfonzo lives two hours away from Mason and Rick. And Dris joined the military. Shortly after his enlistment, the rat pack gathered once more to say a tearful goodbye to Dris, a fallen comrade.

Every year, the guys returned to their alma mater for the seasonal homecoming football game. Tailgating was enjoyable, fun, and highly competitive. At the cookout, these guys displayed their best barbecue skills. When Mason's former best love, Chloe, walked by his tent, his interest in cooking faded. He dropped the spatula and ran after Chloe. Given his Mason Astor style, he didn't waste words. He invited her to dinner, and she accepted. After several dining and reminiscing, they rekindled love and advanced to the altar.

After the marriage, Chloe was under a lot of stress. She had difficulty becoming pregnant. Like her husband's child, she too wanted a son named Mason. She did not intend to be upstaged by Mason's former playmate, Monica, who is also the mother of his namesake.

After years of conception efforts for Chloe, Raysen was born. Four years later, he welcomed his baby brother, Acer. The Astors enjoy the creature comforts of life, which is governed by financial stability. While they have all what they need and more, their spirit is poverty-stricken.

The Progression

Chloe works at Yale Industries. She has been there for eight years. Even though she earns a good salary, her enthusiasm and creativity are diminished. Each morning, it's a struggle getting to work. At the end of the day, mental exhaustion sets in from two culprits, her job and Monica. Chloe relies on bath salts, candles, and a glass of red wine to ease her tension but to no avail. An opportunity emerges, so she courageously applies for another job.

In her most poise posture, she greets, "Good morning, my name is Chloe Miller Astor. I am interviewing for the manager of external sources position."

Ms. Peterson, the administrative assistant, offers her a selection of hot beverages and water as she signs in.

Chloe, girl, you don't have time for clumsiness. You have been waiting on this opportunity. In a gentle tone, she declines a polite Ms. Peterson's offer.

As Chloe takes her seat, she places her designer satchel next to her. Chloe skims through a business magazine. Ms. Peterson stares and smiles. When Chloe lifts her head, they make eye contact. Chloe senses Ms. Peterson wants to engage in a conversation. She returns the magazine to the table as she is complimented on her dress.

Ms. Peterson monopolizes the conversation as they chat about the weather, home football team, and Chloe's least favorite, cooking. Then Ms. Peterson peeks Chloe's interest as she mentions what's it like to work at RAWLY.

She describes December as employee appreciation month. Every Christmas, the partners host a big bash. Mr. Whitmore, lead partner, gives the declaration for the year. He strongly urges them to *forget the former things and neither consider things of old* but to look forward with great expectation to where God is leading them. Tiny red envelopes are issued out, bringing smiles on all their faces like children. It is definitely a magical time of year. The blissful and merry party draws so much attention that even RAWLY competitors want to be on the list of guest names.

As Chloe soaks up the information, her enthusiasm rises. This job would be a tremendous advantage for me. I wonder how many others have interviewed. She remembered being the sixth person to sign in. Chloe was hoping to be first. If so, she could make a stunning impression that would raise the bar for others vying for the position.

Ms. Peterson interrupts while Chloe strategizes internally. She recognizes Chloe from Yale Industries. Her fiancé worked there for five years. When Chloe hears fiancé, she stares at her hand but doesn't see an engagement ring. Then Ms. Peterson corrects herself and says, "Sorry, ex-fiancé." They broke up on Valentine's Day.

"My boyfriend gave me a dozen of red roses, chocolate dipped strawberries, and the most romantic, tear-jerking card I had ever read."

Chloe, trying to look interested, thoughts are racing as to why is this lady telling me all her business. I don't want to hear this. I have my own man issues.

Chloe tilts her head, and Ms. Peterson continues to rant.

"I was deeply moved with his terms of endearment. Then the bottom dropped out when I opened the card. Written in red ink was 'Bailey, you are my sweetest love. Love you forever, Ethan!' Mrs. Astor, I became so enraged."

"Why were you upset?" asks Chloe.

"My first name is Triss. Bailey was supposedly his ex-girlfriend. My faithful Yorkie and I spent the rest of the night eating chocolates and strawberries. Chloe, when you are mistreated before a marriage, it is best to part ways than to expect a metamorphosis that probably will not occur. The signs are always there, but we choose to ignore them. Some boyfriends last, and some pass. I see your husband put a nice ring on your finger."

Chloe gives a slight grin.

"Triss, a few women might agree, it's the size of his heart that really matters. Please call me Chloe."

"Excuse me, Chloe. How can I assist you Mr. Whitmore?"

"Triss, send the next interviewer," he says.

"Chloe, they are ready for you."

William Whitmore, lead partner, introduces himself as he shakes Chloe's hand. He goes around the room, starting to his right are Randolph Seymore, partner, and Darlene Brunswick, supervisor of affairs.

Chloe sits as they review her résumé. Wearing a navy blue dress with navy shoes and a hint of floral perfume, she crosses her legs at the ankles. Darlene facilitates the interview. She has worked at RAWLY for over seventeen years. They are a top ranked company who pride themselves in clients' productivity. Darlene would like to know what distinguishes Chloe from the others and what can she bring to the table.

A confident Chloe elaborates on her college performance and advances to present day.

"I graduated top of my class. For eight years at Yale Industries, my department ranked first in sales and revenues each quarter. Our team created files to link companies to our departments so that we could monitor sales activities simultaneously. Most importantly, we were never in the red. I supervise eight dutiful employees. And I guess you are wondering why I want to leave YI. Well there isn't any room to grow. My growth potential has been stagnant. I've read how RAWLY is a company where the CEO and CFO have a vision beyond tomorrow and next year. I believe in planning for five years, ten years to ensure those coming behind us will have a progressive map, and they can implement whatever fits the era."

Mr. Whitmore, a more subtle older gentleman, has an input that comes out slowly but powerfully.

"Mrs. Astor, I'm thoroughly impressed with the idea of 'progression.' Our vision will take us at least fifteen years up the road. We train and delegate responsibilities as if we are leaving tomorrow. Now don't misunderstand me, I don't have any plans of leaving soon unless my heavenly Father calls me on home. This company was started on Christian principles, and it will stay that way. Our financial integrity is the reason for our success. We believe in sowing and reaping."

After Mr. Whitmore's speech, Chloe was thanked for interviewing. They promise that she'll be informed of their decisions in the coming days ahead. As Chloe exits the interview, she ponders on whether or not her responses were satisfactory.

Immediately, Triss inquires, "How did it go?"

Although she acknowledges Triss' sincerity, Chloe still has doubts because too much is on her mind. Chloe, who has years of experience in corporations, knows it can be who you know and not necessarily what you know.

While getting on the elevator, she is interrupted by a gentleman who recognized her from earlier. He reminds Chloe that he saw her in the elevator. He asks if she works for RAWLY. Chloe bluntly replies, "No, I do not. This is my floor. Have a good day, sir."

When Chloe gets in her car, she wants to share the interview highlights with Mason. She dials him, but her call is forwarded to voice mail. Mason quickly calls Chloe back. He explains how Mason Junior had to be picked up from school. Chloe is confused as to why he picked him up. Tuesday is Monica's scheduled day. Mason told her Monica needs help because she has to work a couple of hours longer.

"Mason, Monica is always needing you for something. I'm not trying to start a fight. I'm just stating facts. If you would tell her no just once, she would stop using you or, better yet, misusing you. Mason, she is playing games, and you can't see it. Please don't give me that sad story about her being the mother of your child. She's a mother all right but not the kind I'm thinking about."

At the end of a long and exhausting day, all Mason could do to reply is sigh. He is not up for a battle. Chloe is not moved by Mason's exhaustive day. She has been tolerating Monica's bag of tricks for too long. Interruptions and distractions are constant vices in their marriage. She wants her husband to sincerely involve himself in her day without prompts. Mason tries to soothe her by addressing the interview.

"Chloe Michelle Miller Astor, how did your interview go? Did you tell anyone you were interviewing?" asks Mason.

"I think it went well. I'm hoping they would call me for the job. But if they don't, I'm still employed at Yale. The only person I told is Sylve."

"Sylve. If you told Sylve, you told everyone. She can't keep her own business. How do you expect her to keep yours? Chloe, hold on a second. Hey, what's up, Monica?"

"Hello, Mason, I really appreciate you getting our son. I will be home around eight. Can you bring him if it's not an inconvenience?" asks Monica.

Mason agrees to drop him and returns to Chloe. "Sorry, bae, that was Monica calling."

"Mason, why do you always have to…forget it. Bye. I'm going to pick up our boys myself while you play games with Monica and her child."

It was Mason's responsibility to get Raysen and Acer until Monica ran interference. Before Chloe gets in the house, Sylve is eager to find out if her best friend got the job. Most importantly, she gives her the latest gossip from Yale Industries.

"Chloe, guess who left the building without giving her dad two weeks' notice? Forget it, I'll tell you. Riley Yale Hawthorne quits effective today. Girl, that no-good, controlling husband made her resign, and Mr. Yale is heartbroken. He told his secretary, Ms. Callahan, to cancel all his appointments for the rest of the week. Drew, who she works alongside every day, didn't know his sister was quitting. How could she not tell her own brother? Drew is upset."

"Chloe, I've known Brett Hawthorne for a long time. He is so narcissistic and controlling. He's always been intimidated by Riley. Mr. Yale tolerates him, but they do not have the best relationship. Although he makes six figures too, his salary is a fraction of hers."

"Girl, ain't no one or nothing will ever be that good to make me, Sylve Amsterdam, drop high six figures and walk away from being next in line to the CEO. Now don't get me wrong, I've had some rather intense moments that made me lose track of my day and time, but no man has ever made me quit my job. I remember this one guy had me trembling but never ever—"

"Okay, Sylve, I get your point," says Chloe.

Sylve continues to sound off about the upheaval at YI. A distraught Mr. Yale is doing all he can to keep his business afloat. With Riley leaving, the most likely candidate will be Channing. Sylve doesn't like Channing. She will be appointed simply because she is Drew's wife. Channing doesn't have business skills. When she visits the office, her concerns are always cosmetic. She is clueless as to the day-to-day operations. Sylve stresses over the idea of her being there.

"Sylve, I would love to talk more, but I have to get in this house and get my kids. Besides, I have bigger issues. I'll talk to you later."

Chloe walks in, and aroma from her mom's cooking is smelled immediately. She loves it when Catherine cooks spaghetti and meatballs. It's her favorite dish as well as her boys'. Although Chloe learned how to cook at an early age, she doesn't care if her domestic skills are ever used.

Chloe knows picking up her boys sometimes means a chastisement. Catherine reprimands her daughter for quick fix days of fast food, drive-through, take a bath, and give good night kisses to her boys.

"Chloe, you were outside for almost half an hour. Put your priorities in order. Your kids ate like they were starving. Y'all li'l corporate American women need to start spending more time at home talking instead of texting with your family."

Chloe squirms as she is being advised by her mother. Catherine constantly opposes Chloe's lifestyle.

"Mom, I feed my boys. I just don't have time to cook, but they eat," says Chloe.

"Do you want to eat, Chloe?" asks Catherine.

"No, you just fed me."

Catherine looks at her daughter and says, "You get that flip mouth from your dad's side."

Chloe's dad is yelling from upstairs. The only words she can hear him say is interview. Chloe is trying to think positively as she talks to her mom about the interview, but she has so much uncertainty. She kisses her good night with thoughts of why her husband suddenly had a change of plans.

The Button

———————————— ✦ ✦✦✦ ✦ ————————————

Mason doesn't understand why he tells Monica no with his mouth and still desires her inwardly. Even though he didn't plan to marry Monica, his resistance toward her is low, and she knows it.

As Chloe enters the house, she tells Raysen and Acer to speak to Mason Junior. This oftentimes infuriates Mason. He wonders why Chloe does not refer to Mason Junior as their brother. He thinks it creates strife in their home. Mason wants all of them to get along but thinks Chloe is antagonistic.

Chloe thinks Mason wants the easy way out by not having a proper perspective. She avoids a fight by going upstairs. She indulges in a long hot bath to soothe away her day's anxieties. Jazz music plays at moderate tone while vanilla scented candles flicker. Mason navigates to Chloe and asks her to wait until he gets back from dropping off Mason Junior. Her husband wants to caress and ease away the stress of her day. He will delicately reach the parts of her that needs his touch. His plan to heighten marital bonds of intimacy is his forte.

Chloe, who is moved with intrigue, wants Mason to hurry up and get back home because she wants everything he has to offer. She reminds herself, there has never been a night when Mason Astor's game didn't end in overtime.

Before Mason leaves to bring his son home, Catherine calls. She forgot to tell Chloe she gave Acer some medicine because he had a stomachache. Mason asks him if his stomach still hurts. A fearful Acer doesn't want to admit he is still in pain. Mason is persistent with his baby boy. He wants to know when it start and how long it's been hurting. Acer tells his dad that his stomach started hurting yesterday. When he got to Nana's house, she gave him some yucky pink stuff. Somehow this didn't ease Mason's mind. He sends Acer and Raysen upstairs to prepare for bed while he brings Mason Junior home. Mason is concerned about Acer but delays discussing it until he returns home.

When Mason Junior gets in the car, he begins to tell his dad that something is bothering him. Mason doesn't give him a chance to express himself by ongoing interrogation of school-related questions. Mason Junior shares his dislike for school and how he hates playing football. He adds that he doesn't have any friends. His mom is always working, and out of nowhere, he drops the question of the day on Mason.

"Dad, I—I—why can't I live with you?" stutters Mason Junior.

Mason tries to keep his eyes on the road while wondering why his son wants to leave home. He hurls question after question to him. Mason Junior is so bombarded that he doesn't know which question to answer. Mason asks if his mother's boyfriend, Scott, is hurting him in any way.

He says, "Dad, his name is Samson. He and Mom broke up last month. She is dating a new guy named Pete."

These answers are not sufficient to Mason. One word is on his mind, and that's "why." As they pull up to the house, Mason Junior pleads with him not to tell. Mason is left wondering what would cause him to leave Monica. Reluctantly, Mason promises to drop the conversation for now.

Monica greets both of them very affectionately, saying they are the two most handsome men on the planet. In every effort to gain Mason's attention, she cannot recognize her son's dissatisfaction. Mason sternly tells her good night. She ignores his good night and offers him to come inside while she bathes. He refuses, but Monica replies with a promise that she will make it good for him and good to him.

"I know Chloe can't give it to you like I can. She's too sophisticated. Every man wants a Monica in the bed. Look at you, Mason, you're imagining it as I say it."

Mason tells her good night over and over. To Monica, those words mean nothing. And she compounds guilt, hoping to make him stay. She adds, "Mason, go home to your family that you love. You don't care anything about us."

"Us," says Mason. "There is no us. I am here for my son. Good night, Monica. Now back away from my car."

As Mason drives up the highway, he visualizes Monica's proposal about sex. She could make him do things he wouldn't normally do. It's like a heroin addiction. But at the end, it isn't worth it.

Rick, one of his best friends from college, calls at the right time. He explains to Rick how Monica is relentless and playing her same games. Mason admits that she would do anything to get him in bed. He also knows Chloe recognizes Monica's tricks, but he cannot tell her because she will make it harder for him to see Mason Junior.

After venting, Rick wants to shoot a few hoops on tomorrow at five-thirty. Before hanging up, Rick tells him to go straight home and don't make any U-turns. Mason shouts out how faithful he is to Chloe. Rick, who knows him best, says, "I know you're faithful, but the best of them can fall."

When Mason pulls up the driveway, Chloe asks him to get the mail. Mason notices how Chloe has been stalking the mailman for the last couple of days. Chloe tells him it's her usual online early Christmas shopping. Their bank account reflects how her shopping is over the limit, and he suggests that she slacks up. After all, half of his closet belongs to her.

When he notices Chloe in her night apparel, he forgets about shopping. He glides up to her and asks, "Are you ready for your man, Dr. Make Me Feel Better?"

Chloe's perfume seeps into his nostrils. As she touches his broad shoulder, she whispers in his ear, "Is my man ready for me?"

Mason looks in her eyes and says, "I'm going prep for your surgery."

Mason is a few steps from the shower when he hears, "Mom! Dad! My tummy hurts!"

Mason runs to Acer's frightful voice.

Acer repeats, "My tummy hurts. My tummy hurts!"

As Mason attempts to touch Acer's stomach, Acer pleads with him to stop.

"Dad! It hurts!" yells Acer.

Mason wants him to point to the area, but Acer refuses to touch it. All he can say is "above my belly button." The words that Acer doesn't want to hear surfaces.

"Son, we will have to go to the hospital."

Raysen, while staring at his younger brother in disbelief, asks his dad what is wrong. Mason is clueless, and so is Chloe. Raysen told his parents how Acer had been complaining about his stomach. Acer didn't want to tell them because he thought it would go away.

Acer lifts his head and tearfully asks, "I'm gonna be okay, huh, Dad?"

"Acer, you are Dad's big boy. You will be just fine," says Mason.

"Hey, Ace Man, you got this," adds Raysen.

Acer tries to say thank you, Raysen, but the only words his brother could hear is Raysen.

Raysen hears Acer call him Raysen. He worries about him because Acer hardly ever calls him Raysen unless it's serious. All of the other times, he calls him Raysee.

While Mason tries to be strong, Chloe calls her parents to meet them at the hospital so Raysen can go home with them. Raysen is determined not to leave his baby brother. He has always been protective of Acer.

Chloe, trying to hold all of them together, keeps saying, "We have to pray and believe that he will be all right."

Acer continually crunches over in pain. Chloe rocks her baby in the back seat of the car. Mason ignores all traffic lights as Acer pleads for him to drive faster.

Once they arrive at the hospital, Acer is too weak to walk. Mason jumps out the car and carries him into the hospital. The night receptionist, who is more interested in cell phone games, nonchalantly asks, "May I help you?"

"My son needs to see a doctor."

Meanwhile, Acer is yelling, "Dad, Dad, help me!"

Mason desperately wants to take her phone and slam it on the floor.

Chloe walks up after parking the car, confused as to why Mason is still at the desk. Mason is hoping to be in a room before Chloe arrives because when it comes to her sons, she is unpredictable. Before Chloe could say a word, a nurse comes for Acer. The receptionist tells Chloe only one person is allowed at a time.

Chloe, with tears flowing, steps closer to her to say, "My son is back there. There is no way you will tell a mother she cannot be with her sick child. I don't give a ——.

"Look, lady. That boy came from me, is a part of me. And I will not leave him. My son is in pain, and he needs his mother, *open that door.*"

The receptionist pushes her phone aside and releases the door for Chloe.

As Acer lays on the bed in a cheerfully decorated room, he begs the nurse not to touch him anymore. With every ouch, she tries to comfort him. Chloe asks how long it will take before the doctor comes.

The door opens.

"I'm Dr. Seagress. Is this Acer Astor?"

"Dr. Seagress, this is our son, Acer. I'm Mason, and this is my wife, Chloe."

Dr. Seagress tells a football joke to lighten the mood. Chloe and Mason smirk, but Acer doesn't. He touches Acer and asks where it hurts? In between sniffs, Acer says, "Above my belly button."

Dr. Seagress has a son his age, so he talks to him about games. He asks him what his favorite sport is while he presses above his belly button.

"Okay, we'll bring you in the back to take some pictures of your stomach. We need to find out what's going on. We'll be right back, Mom and Dad."

Chloe kisses him as he is wheeled off. She turns to Mason with a worried expression.

"Mason, I'm scared. What's happening? Our baby boy is sick. I'm unhappy with my job. To top it off, our marriage is really not where it should be. It's like we are existing but not flourishing."

"Chloe," he says, "let's hope it's a virus or perhaps something he ate. Right now, our attention has to go on Acer. We have to focus on him. Can we discuss the rest later? By the way, I forgot to call my parents. Did your parents arrive?"

Mason calls his mom to inform her of Acer's situation. Lilly blames Acer's sickness on Chloe's cooking and fast food. Mason hopes his mom would end the negative comments, but she continues. Lilly wanted him to marry Monica on the basis of her being pregnant. She advocates for Monica. Lilly's devotion puts a strain on Mason and Chloe's marriage. Monica has always been Lilly's preference for a daughter-in-law. Lilly diverts the conversation to Monica and Mason Junior.

A couple of days ago at the mall, Monica gave Lilly an earful. She persuaded her that Mason is distancing himself from them when they need him most. Lilly firmly believes Chloe is driving a wedge between Monica and Mason. In a harsh tone and still frustrated from the receptionist, he tells his mom to refrain from listening to Monica's exaggerations. He is expecting her to focus on Acer. Mason's dilemma is not a concern to Lilly.

The doctor walks in. This is Mason's excuse to end the call.

Dr. Seagress smiles and says, "I have good news for you. The test did not reveal anything. It could have been a mild stomach virus. A lot of kids been having it lately. I will give him a prescription for pain and orders to follow up with his pediatrician."

While giving a deep sigh of relief, Chloe thanks the doctor. Mason stays in the room while Chloe shares the good news with her parents and Raysen who sits patiently in the waiting area.

The Workbook

The heaviness becomes even more transparent to Chloe. Mason is unable to grasp the unseen, despite its significant impact. Mason's perspective is still in the natural, worldly, the here, and now.

Chloe lays on the bed restless. A million thoughts race through her mind. She shares with Mason what seem to be a roadblock down the path to their intimacy. Both of them know Acer didn't plan his hospital visit. Chloe is aware the problem is deeper. She recommends revisiting a therapist. They have been married for over thirteen years. They decided on three children. It took a long time for the boys to come. Chloe is very grateful for her blessings, but something is still disturbing her spirit.

While in college, Chloe and Mason's relationship was hot and steamy. Even though sexual intimacy was sinful, it was passionate. Nowadays, it's stressful and monotonous.

When Mason recognizes how Chloe is impatiently waiting on a package, he becomes irritated, thinking it's a shopping spree. He discovers it's a package to enhance their relationship. Mason immediately thinks of toys. Chloe purchased a Christian relationship workbook to help recognize barriers and reignite the flame. Perhaps this maybe the panacea to child number three.

Chloe is cognizant the problem isn't medical. They previously sought medical attention. She is doing all she can to alleviate the coldness. After reading a few pages, she murmurs, "Something is not quite right."

Chloe expects his nonverbal reply. But she should have known through times past, Mason struggles with certain issues. With tears rolling down her face, being emotionally and physically exhausted from the hospital ordeal, she repeats, "Something is not quite right."

Mason walks away as he internalizes Chloe's comments. He reverts to his question when they first went to therapy. He quietly asks, "Do I please you, Chloe?"

Mason perceives his manhood is in question. Over and over, he replays how Monica makes him feel and how she is unlimited. But at home, he cannot satisfy his wife. When he is around Monica, his struggles succumb to enticement.

After kissing Mason good night, Chloe senses the coldness piercing through him to the bone. Mason stares at the wall with thoughts of whether the love of his life, the mother of his children, is having an extramarital affair. Is it Jose, whose office is directly across from hers?

Jose constantly wears tight shirts to show off his six-pack. Whenever he leaves out of her office, a trail of cologne lingers behind. Maybe she wanted to leave the company because Jose broke off their affair and found him somebody else.

Is it Rick, the best friend, godparent of his firstborn who is in and out of his house?

Or worse ever, is it Sylve, Ms. Insatiable of the South whose conversations Chloe could not get enough of?

Mason thinks of so many scenarios trying to figure out why. Thoughts are buffering until daylight reflects on the wall. What seems like a few minutes is hours of lies from the enemy playing over and over again.

Before Chloe has a chance to say good morning, Mason interrupts with "I am going check on Acer."

Chloe sits, wondering what's the next phase for their marriage. She intentionally reminisces about their honeymoon years with hopes of being motivated.

Mason mapped out a lifelong marriage until death parts them. He doesn't want her to remarry because another man is not going to spend his money and stay in his house. His idea of marriage and family is for them to have two boys and two girls. He wanted his firstborn son by marriage to have his name (before Monica decided to claim it) so there could be Masons for generations to come.

While that addresses children, he doesn't address the ongoing unmet need of his wife. Chloe knows Mason is a good man with lots of untapped potential. But she struggles to discover the root cause and identify barriers. She ponders on whether therapy would alleviate the burdens and uproot absurd mental images of her being unfaithful.

As Mason steps back into the bedroom, both minds reroute to Acer. Acer is not in pain, but Mason wants Chloe to follow through with his pediatrician, Dr. Turray.

"Chloe, keep me informed of Acer's appointment. Also, if you don't mind, can you please drop off Grandma Lera's checks to her? I was supposed to give them to her the other day," says Mason.

Chloe gets dressed and prepares breakfast for him and the boys. Mason hurries out the house and decides to pick up breakfast on his way to work. Chloe tries to extend their conversation, but it is interrupted with "Umm, Chloe, we'll talk later." Chloe feels slighted as Mason hugs and kisses his boys before leaving the house. He tells Raysen to look after his brother. It is an easy assignment for Raysen because the love he has for Acer is unparallel. Chloe stands in the kitchen, expecting a kiss, and all she gets is a goodbye wave.

Chloe, needing affection, reverts to her boys who hugs her as they leave for school. She thanks them because if even for that moment, her emptiness is alleviated by her sons.

A baffled Mason tries to put other things on his mind. He calls Rick to make sure their basketball game is still on. Rick assures him and reminds his friend to warm up his old bones. Rick knows a label "old" would strike a nerve in Mason. In Mason's eyes, he has the body of a twenty-five-year-old with a four-pack. He figures four out of six ain't never bad since he still qualifies as eye candy.

Mason asks Rick to hold on because Monica is calling. Rick is perturbed and shakes his head. Rick knows caution has to be exercised. If Mason isn't careful, being involved with Monica is like putting *fire in your bosom*.

Mason reluctantly answers her but dictates telling her it better be about their son. Monica knows when Mason is uptight.

Monica, with sarcasm, asks, "Is there trouble in paradise, Mason Phillip Astor Sr.?"

Mason totally disregards the questions. Monica's jealousy of Chloe and determination to win Mason back is ever present. She crosses boundaries to find out if Mason's attitude is resulting from a lack of love, labeling Chloe as pretty and poise who didn't give her husband any loving last night.

Monica rationalizes only a lack of love would have Mason so frustrated early in the morning. Candidly, she brings up the past as to how and when Mason Junior was conceived, boldly announcing to Mason his affection and love for her are genuine and that it wasn't the alcohol. Her fantasy includes Mason wanting her, and even to this day, he can still have her.

"Mason, you want me, all of me. And you can have me. And I'm still yours. Why don't you come on over and get some good morning love? Your frustration would slip away. I can guarantee a smile by noon or a rain check for a replay. FaceTime me. Let me give you a sneak preview of what's to come."

"Monica, what's your reason for dialing me?"

Monica said with a seductive tone, "I'm telling you why I'm calling. I want you to tell me when and how. I take that back. Mason, if you tell me when, I will tell you how."

Mason is growing weary of Monica's games. All he wants to hear is that his son is doing okay. Once he gets that assurance, he is prepared to end the conversation. Since Monica didn't get the results she hopes for, she resigns to lying and telling him she is just playing with him.

Aware of Mason's single focus, Monica schemes by inviting him to their son's football practice. She advocates for Mason Junior using football as an alibi to conceal her motive. A deceitful Monica describes Mason as supportive. Her friends suggest she obligates him to court-appointed child support. She refuses to get the courts involve because he is there when she needs him, and he freely pays for Mason Junior's expenses.

Mason is unable to detect the pretentious acts. When Monica strokes his ego with flattery, he promises that he will be at practice.

Mason sits in his car listening to jazz, pondering on his issues. He is unaware how a planned few minutes quickly becomes an hour. He walks in the building, greets his secretary, Brenda, with a sub-dued good morning. He is not mentally prepared to work. Brenda relieves his burden with good news. His meeting with Mr. Reynolds is rescheduled for next week.

Mason expounds on his support for Mason Junior's football practice to her. His son is trying out for the same team as Brenda's nephew, Foster. Foster's dad, Mike, is determined he receives a full ride to college. Mike is a sports enthusiast. He would love to see Foster advance to the NFL. Prep-Con Academy would be the school for Foster to get media coverage.

Prep-Con Academy has an awesome record. They won the championship the last four years. Brenda asked Haley, who works on the second floor at Pencale, to put in a good word for Foster. Haley's dad is Coach Brunson. Brenda tells Mason that she texts Haley often. Haley gave her word that she would talk to her dad. Brenda promises to advocate for Mason Junior also. Mason is appreciative but knows his son doesn't have an interest in the game. Monica is pushing him to play. Mason is conflicted as he remembers his son's desires to leave home.

The Secret

Grandma Lera tries to mentor Chloe into becoming a kingdom woman who is effective and essential anywhere. Chloe's confidence and security are linked to their bank account.

Grandma Lera is the stabilizing force in the family. Chloe's visits to her are always encouraging. Even though she is Mason's maternal grandmother, she loves Chloe dearly.

When Chloe enters the house, they embrace and chat over a cup of coffee. Chloe forgets the checks are in her purse when she notices a new keepsake frame on the table. It has a golden twenty-five raised on the right corner.

Grandma Lera sips and smiles. "Chloe, I thought you knew."

She embarks down memory lane to explain its significance. For the longest, she claimed twenty-five as her golden number. When she was twenty-four years old, she was crossing a street downtown. Lera Waters wearing a beautiful white dress with purple flowers, caught Joe's attention. He and his friends were standing on the sidewalk as she crossed the street. He smiled, then he ran up to her and said, "You are the most beautiful woman in the world, and you have the prettiest legs."

She didn't let him see her blush as she walked away. Her strut gave all of them something to talk about. She started twisting, and the rest is history. They fell in love and were married the next year on her twenty-fifth birthday.

Even to this day, he compliments her legs and beauty. She knows they don't look like they used to, but in his eyes, they are just as beautiful as the first day he saw them. First words in their relationship were important because they will always be remembered. Kind, compassionate, and loving words, according to Joe, are the foundation for their marriage. Every fall, he plants hydrangeas, pansies, and lilies. Those flowers are a constant reminder how God blessed him with a good wife.

Grandma Lera pinpoints some crucial life principles to Chloe. She unfolds how their marriage, through ups and downs, survives. She bridges the gap of their ages by exemplifying a man's needs. Her prime example is, after marrying Joe, she never wears pants. It's not because she is old school or forbidden. She wears dresses to refresh Joe's memory of who and what he loves.

Chloe assumes she has arthritis because she keeps rubbing cream in the house. Rubbing her legs are Joe's simple pleasure. She refuses to rob him of his duty. Every night before they go to bed, he reaches for an inexpensive $3.57 cream. He is fulfilling his needs and hers in the absence of sex.

Hopefully, Chloe will realize love, agape love, doesn't always have to advance to exchanging bodily fluids. And it surely doesn't require expensive clothing. Intimacy in their marriage is a connection of soul and spirit. He belongs to her, and she belongs to him.

She knows Joe only has eyes for her. His soul and spirit connect and intertwine with her. She fills his innermost being with respect and loyalty, and it gives him great satisfaction. One hundred women can walk in front of him, but none of them will look better than his precious Lera. As Chloe drinks her coffee, she hopes to one day soon gain the same affection and faithfulness.

Chloe could listen to Grandma Lera talk about marriage for hours. The conversations are rejuvenating and inspiring. To Chloe, they have a strong bond that cannot be broken. Grandma Lera, in simple terms, classifies it as "unity." Life experiences have trained them to look to God, instead of the world, when problems arise. She can attest that he has never failed to help them, and he won't.

Strife and confusion can destroy a marriage, but poor communication and negative thoughts will kill it at the root. Some minds can't change, especially if they are prone to negativity. It doesn't matter if truth manifests. Some folks believe the lies of their mind.

Grandma Lera, an octogenarian, is being transparent. Her method of mentoring is to help Chloe and Mason avoid the pitfalls of life. She is still cognizant of the games. Her motto is, "Young ladies may try to trap men with sex. It might get them, but it won't keep them." She emphasizes how real connection has to occur in the spirit where God resides.

She elaborates on Mason's upbringing in church. She had tremendous influence on him as a child. As Grandma Lera pours another cup of coffee, she tells Chloe, "I had the opportunity to instill biblical truths in Mason. But as he grew older, they have become dormant."

Chloe asks, "When will he use them? Where are they?"

Chloe is overwhelmed and unable to give Mason her full attention. Sometimes she feels like relinquishing it all. Grandma Lera detects her frustration. Chloe hears a confident "everything will be all right." She gives a slight nod and reaches Grandma Lera her checks.

"Thanks for bringing them over. Chloe, my overprotective grandson doesn't like them being delivered to my mailbox. I don't like using that plastic card. It tempts you to spend more money. When I write checks, I keep up with my money better, and it helps me to save more. I notice how people swipe that card, and it becomes an addiction. Some people swipe, swipe, and swipe some more," Grandma Lera explained.

"When I am in the grocery store, the cashier and the people in line behind me are mad because it takes more time to write a check. When I see them twitch, I write even slower. One time I had a young man behind me. He was huffing, making all sorts of gestures. I wrote the check for the wrong amount intentionally. The cashier said very rudely, 'Ma'am this ain't right.' I told her, 'Oh, I'm sorry. I'll write you another one.' The young man asked, 'How much her groceries cost?' She told him $37.56. He reaches the cashier his card. I said, 'Oh bless you, young man.' He shook his head and mumbled, 'Don't worry about it.' I laughed all the way to the car."

Chloe laughs. "Grandma Lera, you are a mess."

"I may be old but I'm not a fool."

She challenges Chloe to put her card away for twenty-one days. Without shopping, hopefully a sense of value on the important aspects of life will take precedence. If nothing else, she wants Chloe to remember to keep life simple. Grandma Lera and Joe have been married for over sixty years. If Chloe and Mason would allow God to lead, they will get there.

Chloe is pessimistic about their future. She knows something is wrong and expresses it to Mason constantly. There is something she just can't explain. Grandma Lera suspects uncertainty. She offers Chloe words of wisdom.

"If you can't see a problem, then it's spiritual," she says.

Chloe recounts the cohesive moments in the early stages of their marriage. They were airtight, and nothing and no one could come in between them. Then one day, she notices a change. And it's like they are slowly spiraling downward.

"Chloe, there are a lot of people with open wounds. Lilly is my daughter, and I love her dearly. Joe and I did everything to give Lilly and Elizabeth a good education. We sacrificed our personal needs so they could have what they needed and wanted. Sometimes I feel we gave them too much. As a wife and mother, I tried to make up for their older brother."

"Brother? Grandma Lera did you say brother? Who? Where is he?" asks Chloe.

Grandma Lera reaches for the sugar and says, "His name is Joseph Allen Pruitt III, our firstborn child. When he was two years old, he became ill. They thought it was a cold, but he had pneumonia."

She checked on him in the middle of the night. He laid in the bed calm, no movement. The room was still. She looked at the clock, and it was 2:14 a.m. As she picked up his lifeless body, her heart skipped a beat, and the tears flowed.

She rocked her baby for hours. Joe got up and came in the room to check on them. When he walked in, silence and tears flooded the room. He didn't say anything. Words were left unspoken. He turned around, and the next person she saw was the coroner. Joe wanted him buried the very next day. She can still feel the pain in her heart. She slept in that room for months, and Joe avoided it for months. Whenever she sees 2:14 a.m. or p.m. on a clock, chills come over her. Their firstborn son was gone.

With compassion, Chloe says, "Grandma Lera, I am so sorry. I'm thinking about how we could have lost Acer."

"Some pains cut really deep, and you wonder if you'll ever get well. We had to bury our baby."

Chloe was very curious and asks, "How did the both of you heal?"

"My healing came in a dream. I was in a beautiful greenfield. There were bright flowers all around. As I walked, I noticed a child running toward me. He was wearing a white T-shirt and blue shorts, carrying flowers in his hand. When he got close to me, his facial features were a blur. He reached me the flowers and smiled. I said, 'Thank you. They are beautiful.' He said, 'I picked these roses for you.' After reaching me the roses, the thorns scratched his hand, and it bled. I tried to wipe his hand, but he stopped me. 'It'll stop,' he said. 'We don't hurt here.' The next few words spoken by the child healed my grief-stricken soul. He said, 'Mama, I'm not sick anymore.' I cried and knelt in a pool of my own tears. Then he ran away from me. As he turned around, I saw the number eight on his back. Then I woke up. I wanted to tell Joe that I saw our son, but he had already gotten up."

"What did the eight represent?" Chloe asks.

"Eight is a number of beginning. Without a doubt, he had begun life in the presence of Jesus. The next morning after the dream, I went to the kitchen and poured a cup of coffee. Joe was chopping lumber in the backyard. Suddenly I heard an earth-shattering scream. I jumped up and ran to the backdoor. Joe was on the ground, sobbing uncontrollably. I held him, and he held me. We had been released from our individual private pain. From that moment on, life came back to us."

One year later, Lillian was born, then Elizabeth came a year after her. Those girls put the light back in Joe's eyes. She is sharing this so Chloe would not waste time living life frivolously. She needs to live healed and delivered. When people keep secrets, it only makes them sick. If they are emotionally sick, then they become sicker. Problems turn into pain, which can result in a sin-sick soul.

"But how could all this affect your grandson?" wonders Chloe as she tries to connect the dots.

Grandma Lera picks up the photo album and points to Lilly's baby picture.

"Well Mason is unsettled," says Grandma Lera, pointing back to the picture referring to Lilly. "His unsettling is a direct link to his mother. Lilly is greatly loved, but she caused us a lot of grief."

Chloe has been like a granddaughter to them ever since she became a part of the family. Grandma Lera is very comfortable disclosing family secrets. It is not to belittle Lilly or even Mason. She knows you have to get to the root rather than merely treating the symptoms.

"Tell me, when was the last time you all went to church?" she asks.

"Hmm, about two weeks ago. Grandma Lera, we go on a regular basis."

"Okay, but don't go because it's on your 'things to do' list. Go to grow. I don't ever want the Astors to be one of those families who look like they got it all together."

Chloe knows exactly what she meant. A guilty image of them walking in church well-groomed emerges, but deep within, there isn't a real connection with the Lord—the Astors sitting in church stiff, going to check off the attendance box. When worship service is over, they hop in the clean car, go get something to eat, return home, and it repeats the next week or the week after.

An intimate relationship with God is needed so they can develop godly children. Chloe thinks her version of praying suffices until it is explained in-depth. Grandma Lera expounds how prayer is talking to God and taking time to listen to what he has to say.

"Prayer is more than giving our heavenly Father a wish list then adding in Jesus's name like it's magic," she declares.

Chloe welcomes the loving correction from her. Mason gives either criticism or correction but not out of love. It makes her dry inside. The truth illuminates because some men can't give you what they don't have or don't know. Mason is a man on the outside. But deep within, he is a boy that needs maturing and spiritual developing. Hurting people hurt other people. If they would put God first, their house will get better.

Grandma Lera would always hope and pray for her precious Lillian, but she hasn't seen it manifest yet. She is not giving up on her. They named her Lillian Olivia Pruitt because after the tragedy of losing a son, God blessed them with another child. Lilly was born at 2:15 a.m., Easter Sunday morning.

The Matthews, who lived next door to them, had a son born the same month as theirs. They named him Dome. He was like an older brother to Lilly and Elizabeth. He would go by the house and help Joe all the time. Dome would not let the girls go out on a date unless he went too. He would sit a couple of rows behind them at the movies. Dome was very protective of them but disapproved of Lilly's boyfriend.

35

When Lilly was about to graduate from high school, she fell in love with the Stern's son. Henry Stern owned the general store in town. He and Margaret had three children: Beth, Ann, and Nash. Nash was head over heels in love with Lilly. He would drop off a bag of groceries at their backdoor. Back then, it isn't safe at all for blacks and whites to talk, let alone date. Joe begged Lilly to break things off. But she kept sneaking around with Nash.

One Friday night, leaving the juke joint, Dome and his brother were jumped by several white men. They threatened to kill Dome and Lilly and burn the house down if Lilly didn't leave Nash alone. Dome's right arm was broken, and his brother was severely beaten. The sheriff's daughter was madly in love with Nash. They knew it was Sheriff Jones and some of his friends that beat them. They couldn't report the sheriff to the sheriff.

Dome was very angry, but Lilly didn't care. All she knew was Nash. Although he sincerely loved Lilly, it wasn't healthy. Dome and Lilly stopped speaking. Lilly continued to date Nash.

Shortly after, his parents sent him to college in Boston, but he didn't want to go. Nash didn't want to be in Boston. He quit school and joined the navy. Lilly was heartbroken. To add insult to injury, Lilly, while home on break from college, had changed drastically. She was pregnant and tried to hide it. Nash didn't know about the baby, but somehow his mom found out. Mrs. Margaret came over to the house to ask Lilly to raise the baby if it was white. Lilly refused.

After Mrs. Margaret left, Lilly saw Dome visiting his parents next door. She went over to see him and apologize. Dome ignored her. Lilly kept begging, but Dome walked away. Lilly ran behind him and tripped on a plank. She didn't think anything was wrong until later that night.

While lying in the bed, she yelled for help. Blood was everywhere, and she lost the baby. Dome wasn't to blame, but he still felt that if he had listened then maybe she wouldn't have tripped.

Lilly wanted the baby. She didn't see Nash until years later. His parents lied to him about Lilly. They told him she had married Dome. This happened while Nash was in the service. Whenever he came back on his seldom visits, he would leave a bag of groceries by the backdoor.

One day, it was Thanksgiving holiday, two bags of groceries were left. Those bags were an indication Nash found out about the baby. Lilly stopped coming home. They didn't see her for Thanksgiving or Christmas. She would call and write plenty of letters.

"Mom and Dad," she said, "my job is keeping me very busy. I hope to see y'all soon. Thanks for your support. Love, Lilly."

She had sunken into depression that her parents were all too familiar with. Nevertheless, there was still something different about her.

Joe figured Lilly needed time to adjust with hopes of her coming around, but Grandma Lera knew differently. They didn't see her until the end of summer.

It was the following year when Lilly met Carter. He pursued her for a year. He would yell by her dorm room window and meet her after class. His persistence paid off. Lilly finally gave in the next year. They started dating. After graduation, they decided to marry.

Six months later, Lilly was pregnant with Carter Junior. Mason and Leon were born two years apart.

Chloe's posture changes as she takes all this in.

Carter and the boys didn't know about the baby. A parents' secrets can affect their children. Lilly needs to release this so she can be free. Sometimes, most times, she is bitter and mean-spirited. Carter loves Lilly more than she loves him. If he knew, he wouldn't care. Carter feels powerless against Lilly.

Although she is the love of his life, Lilly's fractured past keeps her weighed down. Carter is unable to connect the pieces of her life. Lilly does not appreciate him. Lilly lives for Lilly. Selfish people only seek to receive, and they do it with entitlement.

As a result, CJ, Mason, and Leon were raised in a house that was never a home. It is a dry place, even when they gathered for holidays. Joy and laughter are subdued. Lilly is discontented and garmented in bitterness and does not realize it. Those decades of ungodly attitudes have her shackled and blind as to how it affects not only her but also her family.

Although, Lilly is consistent in her church attendance, her devotion is superficial. For a woman her age, sadly enough, church is a regimen rather than a relationship with God.

Chloe's phone rings while history unfolds.

"Hello, Chloe, this is Triss from RAWLY. Mr. Whitmore would like to know if you are available to come in and meet with them tomorrow at ten forty-five?"

"Yes, Triss, I will be there."

Chloe is excited to have a second interview but has doubts that the job is hers. Her faith is not intact.

"Grandma, sometimes I believe then sometimes I don't."

"Chloe, all things are possible if you believe. You need a made-up mind. You can't be pregnant for three months, then later you say I don't think I'm pregnant. Your words have power, dear. If you don't want it, don't believe it. And speak it," she adds.

Somehow Chloe knows the truth she hears is in the Bible. Grandma suggests she opens that fancy phone and read it for herself.

"The Bible is not a boring book. It's a manual for living your best, victorious life. If advice is taken from social media, why not believe the Bible? There will be *no new thing under the sun*. It may have a different name, but believe me, it is not new. Now get out of here. I have taken up enough of your time. I'll tell Joe you came by. He's at the feed store," says Grandma Lera.

The Court

Mason is conflicted. It is of his own doing. Although he graduated from college, Mason is cemented in a developmental stage. Some decisions are painful because Mason struggles with truth.

Chloe decides to call Mason. She knows he was annoyed when he left the house. She wants to inform him of Acer's appointment for tomorrow at two fifteen but didn't want it to run interference with her second interview at RAWLY. Chloe's first priority is Acer.

Mason briefly listens to Chloe and casually delays their conversation for another time. He is on the basketball court with Rick. Mason hopes this game would be a great stress reliever. He has so much on his mind. He apologizes to Rick for being late. Mason Junior's football practice took longer than expected. Without hesitation, he informs Rick of his drama. Instantly, Rick knows Monica is the culprit.

Mason explains the football dilemma. His son complains about the heat, homework, being tired, and how he doesn't have any friends. He doesn't want to play, but Monica is forcing him. Monica is unappreciative. Monica is always calling. And worst of all, Mason is in the middle of the mess without a remedy.

Rick is hearing Monica, Monica, Monica. So he tries to lift Mason's burden with a tad bit of playful mockery.

"I wonder if your son is a chip off the old block."

When Mason hears the word *old*, he quickly becomes defensive. Rick detects the seriousness and starts to laugh.

"Man, you are uptight, calm down. I'm just joking."

Mason apologizes for being defensive. "I have so much going on right now. There is trouble all around me. Trouble in my home, trouble with my son, trouble with Monica. Where does it end?"

Rick knew Monica had to be the source. He is confrontational yet sensitive to Mason. Mason unloads on his friend.

"Monica will not stop."

This fiasco has been occurring on and off since Mason Junior was born. Monica is relentless in her pursuit of him. She has the backing of Lilly who advocates for her. Monica plays the victim role very well. When Mason didn't marry her, Lilly was upset. Monica presented her version as if they were madly in love, and he proposed to her. Her parents told Lilly that Mason broke the engagement off and left their daughter pregnant to raise a child alone. His dad knew better, but Lilly thought he should have married Monica.

Mason deeply regrets getting involved with her, but he can't rid her out of his head. All he has to say is yes, and she will let him sleep with her. The simplicity of a yes comes easy. There is an open door. Rick can only pray that he closes it. It has absolutely nothing to do with Mason Junior. Mason is attracted to deception. And if he sleeps with her, God forbid, his marriage is over. Chloe will be the first to know because Monica will boast and post. He is being misguided to think she can give him what he can't get at home without having a price to pay. He is running to lust as he runs from love. This time, if he succumbs to his weakness, he can't blame it on alcohol.

Mason has allowed her to get too deep in his spirit. The scenes from yesteryears with Monica replay constantly. He isn't as strong as he thinks. His thoughts of her are on the forefront. They will come, but it's up to him to disregard them.

Mason questions, "Rick, why do some women make it so easy for a brother? If a woman doesn't place value on herself, why should a man? I mean, they know you are married, and yet they still will give it up. If I was a woman, I would keep myself pure until marriage."

Rick already knows the answer. Their collegiate days were mostly good times. Mason still has some of those schemes running through his veins. The question Mason should ask is not why some women make it easy but rather why men can't say no.

Monica wouldn't care if he never leaves Chloe. All she wants from him is a few stolen moments, and she would feel victorious. The spite would uplift her self-esteem. A few minutes compared to permanent is a cheap exchange of selling yourself short but not for Monica. She believes it provides perpetual happiness.

Mason, unrealistically, expects Monica to change. Then on the other hand, he thinks Chloe is tripping. She keeps telling him something is wrong in their marriage. Rick strongly encourages him to pay attention and listen to his wife. Women, who seeks God's guidance, can spot trickery a mile away.

Monica will not make it easy for him. Mason always wanted a good, respectful woman. He delights in someone who will love him, but it isn't reciprocated. Andrew told Rick and the other men at Brotherhood Connection meeting, "If a man gets love, it will foster faithfulness, respect, and compassion. But when he gets it, he doesn't know what to do with it, especially the man who has dealt with a lot of women. They bring a game mentality into marriage."

Rick summarizes some of their meeting discussions.

"Spirituality and carnality cannot coexist. Godly men know how to make love to their wives without taking off their clothes. If all you can offer a woman is sex, two texts, and a meal, you are empty. Money and sex can tie you to ill-fated women, and months later you will wonder how you got involved. Then you will wonder why you can't get loose."

He is all for them hanging out on the court, but he wants his friend to grow spiritually. He has been inviting him to Brotherhood Connection at church. The meetings are awesome and empowering. They come together to strengthen each other.

In Mason's ear, Rick sounds like Chloe. She has been pleading for more church involvement. Rick knows Chloe is right, but he is not sure if Mason knows she is right. He will need spiritual tools to fight and win this war.

Rick didn't escape his struggles. He and his wife endured lots of hardship. Giselle credits their success to surrendering to the will of God. When they inquired of the Lord how to make their marriage reflect him, they flourish. Rick knows his wife trusts him and has their best interest at heart. They don't have hidden plans.

In the meantime, Mason could only dream of a relationship like theirs. Rick explains how he intercedes for Giselle whenever there's a need. He does it discretely and rejoices when his prayer is answered. He knows what she needs. For the areas he can't fulfill, God fills the void. He is not only her lover but her prayer partner.

"Mason, what are Chloe's nonmaterial needs?"

Mason stutters and pauses.

"I cannot think of anything. She has everything."

"Mason, your wife has needs other than shopping. If you can't name them, you aren't fulfilling them."

Rick learned to manifest the heart of God toward Giselle. In doing so, he saw significant improvement.

Rick tells him, "Bro, we are not in college anymore. This marriage covenant is about love, trust, and compromising with each other."

As Rick stares at the jerseys hanging in the gym, he remembers when his time, attention, texts, and most importantly, conversations were given to everyone else. Meanwhile his marriage was deteriorating. He used to believe it was harmless to text until he realized the dangers involved. A hand wave, hello, or any emoji to another woman was creating an emotional affair. If he couldn't tell his wife, then it wasn't right. Being convicted by the spirit empowered him to close doors permanently. Now he reserves that time and energy for Giselle, and he reaps bountifully.

Brotherhood Connection meetings taught him this and more. Marriage will never ever work if you are selfish and bitter, especially if you don't know it. It didn't matter how bad it got between him and Giselle, he never made the mistake and slept with another woman. It would have caused substantial regrets. He encourages Mason to focus on a godly lifestyle.

"Rick, I feel like I don't know where to turn. I think all sorts of crazy, negative thoughts," says Mason.

"Mason, you are trying to fight a spiritual battle with your flesh, and you are losing. Give yourself to God. Let go."

When they were in college, they partied and did some damnable stuff. The rat pack enjoyed each other's company, but Jeff and Alfonzo are still talking nonsense. They got the same game but different players. Rick knows Mason is stuck in those flirtatious days of eyeing women when they walk pass, taking a virtual tour from head to toe.

Rick continues, "Man, you can't have every woman you see, and every woman is not after you. You ought not think so highly of yourself. It is time for us to mature and be godly examples to our children. You are a legend in your own mind."

Mason puts his head down in shame as he realizes the truth is being told. Although some of it is bitter, better are wounds from a friend than kisses from an enemy.

Rick discloses his most recent spiritual attack. He says, "Last week at work, this girl approached me. She said, 'If you buy me lunch, I can make it a happy meal.' I told her, 'Why should I settle for fast food when my prime rib is at home?' She said a few choice words and walked away. *If you resist the devil, he will flee.*"

Rick asks, "Mason, when was the last time you did something special for Chloe?"

"I do it all the time. She orders it, the mailman delivers, and our bank account is depleted," brags Mason.

"Bro, what she does for herself, whether your money or hers, is for her. When did you do something for her that came from you, your heart?" he asks.

Lilly barges in with a phone call at a very crucial moment. After briefly inquiring about the kids, she makes her point clear. Monica informs her of the upcoming football game, and she wants to be there. Mason knows if he continues to entertain his mom, it will frustrate him. His crisis is more important than Lilly's babbling.

"Man, Monica keeps in contact with my mother too much. I try to tell her that Monica and I were not dating. It was just alcohol and sex. I will tell anyone who drinks, don't drink brown. Years later it will make you frown. I woke up the next morning, and the bottle was empty."

"Mason, I understand. Sometimes I wonder if somebody will knock on my door and say, 'Surprise.' It all seemed like fun and good times until I looked back. I realize it was nothing but a setup from the devil to destroy my future. If I would have taken heed to my parents, my troubles would be few," confesses Rick.

The rat pack would tease guys who weren't having sex. They called them nerds. Now they wish they would have been the one being teased. There is nothing in the past that they want or need. Mason is trying to find a way to get his head in this marriage game. But doubt in many forms arises. Sometimes he wonders if he is really in love with Chloe. He loves her but not sure if he is in love with her. He questions his love and devotion openly.

Rick details, "Mason Astor, my friend, my brother, love or in love is a cop-out. People use that as an excuse to have an affair and justify their actions. All of a sudden it's 'I love you but I'm not in love with you.' Where did that come from? Point blank, either you love me or you don't. Just that simple. God loves us."

"Yes, there are different types of love, *agape, eros, storge,* and *phileo,* but that crap of in love, a side love, a top love, around love, 30 percent love, seventy-five love is an excuse to sin. Either you're all in, or you're not. Keep it one hundred, and you can't go wrong."

He continues, "People who want to tip out of their marriage to satisfy Ms. or Mr. FEAR use that love alibi."

Mason is confused. He wants to know who is Mr. or Ms. FEAR.

Rick explains, "FEAR is false evidence appearing real. Whoever you join yourself to that is not God-appointed is not the real deal. They are false and temporary. You think she is gratifying your flesh, but her real assignment is to distract and devour."

"Actually, she has penetrated your spirit because fear is a spirit. You have connected with a soul tie that God never planned for you. To break it off requires praying and sometimes fasting. Your four- or six-pack cannot help you cut this one off."

Mason is being pulled in so many directions. The dilemma occurs when he desires flesh's choice and still wants the benefits of God's choice and expect both of them to cohabitate peacefully. He is saved, and Rick believes it. But that doesn't stop the enemy from throwing darts. The enemy studies him. The words that come out of Mason's mouth invites the devil.

Although he has been in love with Chloe, he knows she could have chosen any man on campus. Rick petitions him, "Mason, you got to find a way, a godly way, to get your marriage on the right path."

They didn't get a chance to play ball, but Rick much rather he works on his marriage than his muscles. Before they leave off the court, Rick gives him a few more pointers.

He adds, "Remember, Chloe, and no other woman, can give you what you need to get from God. You have to go to him for your-self. There isn't a spirit that can make a person whole like the Holy Spirit. If a married couple cannot connect within their spirit, one of you will experience unfulfillment. No private part or amount of money will ever satisfy."

We are accustomed to our flesh and its desire. We see a woman, and immediately we think or say something about her shape or bulging parts. But when it comes to our heavenly Father, we struggle to praise and love Him."

When Rick learned to love God, truly love God and listen to him, Giselle kept pinching him, asking if he is all right. He is a changed man. There is harmony, peace, and joy in their home. They still laugh at silly things. There are times they disagree, but they don't allow strife. Both of them will have opposite views, but they leave it with God. Eventually, one of them will apologize. Apologizing is not weakness. It demonstrates his inner strength.

For Mason, things are rough now, but he is being encouraged to try. Some problems are self-inflicted. When he sows, he forgets that he will reap. Mason feels like he has been knocked out in the first round but is determined to go home and self-evaluate.

Chloe observes the perplexity on Mason when he arrives home. She asks how the game was and if she could have his undivided attention.

Mason replies "We just hung out."

She wonders that if RAWLY offers her the job, would it require more hours? And are they in a position to handle extra time away from home? Mason thought Chloe is referring only to the boys. He knows that is an easy fix. But Chloe is concerned about their marriage, whether or not this job would put a strain on it.

Mason, effortlessly says to Chloe, we will get through this.

The Manager

Chloe has been discontented at YI for many years, but stress distracts her. She is cognizant about how the games are played in corporate arenas. There are moments when you just have to "jump" because you can't wait for them to give it to you. You have to get it for yourself. God does order our steps, but we have to walk.

Chloe returns to RAWLY for a second interview. The gentleman who was in the elevator last week, greets her again.

Chloe doesn't recognize him but cordially asks, "Can you press seventh floor please?"

He tells her his name is Jonathan. After saying, "We meet again."

Chloe doesn't remember him but introduces herself as Mrs. Astor. Jonathan wants to know if she works for RAWLY. Chloe didn't give a definitive response.

But Jonathan interprets it as optimistic and says, "When you get the job, swing by office 508. I work for Turner-Root. I will treat you to a cup of coffee in the café downstairs. Good luck, and I hope to see you around."

When she arrives at the office, Triss greets her and notifies Mr. Whitmore. While waiting to be called in, Chloe prays silently and asks God to lead her. If this is his will, let it be done. If this position will cause division in her home, close the door. At the end of her prayer, Triss summons her to the interview.

Mr. Whitmore begins by stating how pleased they are she accepted the second interview. He introduces Thomas Radcliff, partner; Laura Cruznik, director; and Mike Prawls, CFO. They were absent for the initial interview. Darlene and Randolph, who were at the first interview, are also in the room. Mr. Whitmore alerts the team to Chloe's impressive résumé. He mentions how her references spoke very highly of her. William smiles about her polished reputation.

Darlene reaches Chloe a sheet that details RAWLY's sales and growth patterns. She places great emphasis on the company's value of respect. Offenses of any sort are not tolerated and should be reported immediately. She says their team has come to an agreement.

She highlights, "Chloe Astor, you have been offered the job as manager of external sources."

Immediately a calm peaceful spirit is upon Chloe. Inwardly she tells God, "Thank you."

Darlene presents Chloe their company's packet. The packet details salary, job description, 7 percent bonus and 3 percent merit increase. When Chloe hears 7 percent bonus and 3 percent merit increase, she imagines dollar signs flying everywhere. She could hardly contain herself.

Darlene continues to specify the months in which bonuses and increases will be distributed, but Chloe is already shopping. After Darlene says that the other bonus is separate from the 7 percent, Chloe realizes she missed an important detail. She asks Darlene to please repeat the last bonus. Darlene explains how each year the partners distribute lagniappe Christmas bonus. Chloe is totally amazed. While working at Yale, bonuses and increases were far and in between.

Her final instructions to Chloe require her to review the packet. She has twenty-four hours to sign and accept with a start date not to exceed fifteen days. Chloe is eager and willing to sign. The Christmas bonus made the offer extra sweet.

Chloe is confident this is the right move. Darlene's explanation of the company's policy provides reassurance. RAWLY is the type of company that doesn't want their employees stressed or overwhelmed. They place high markings on teamwork.

Chloe sincerely thanks them for the opportunity. She makes a declaration that her work performance will match their confidence in her abilities.

Chloe is pleased to tell Triss they will be coworkers.

Triss discloses, "I already knew. I'll show you which office is yours. You will meet everyone when you start. Just a reminder, you will have twenty-four hours to submit the policy and salary acceptance. When do you want your twenty-four hours to start?"

"At 2:00 p.m. Triss, thanks again for your encouragement. I look forward to working with you."

As Chloe gets on the elevator, Jonathan is there again. She asks if his job is on the elevator. Jonathan told her it is his lucky day. He gets to meet the woman of his dreams, again. Chloe kindly expressed that she is a married woman with two handsome boys.

"I can give you one more," he says.

"My husband would not approve of me cheating."

"Then don't tell him. He doesn't have to know anything. How do you know he isn't cheating?" replies Jonathan.

She wonders why she is entertaining Jonathan. She exits the elevator and waves bye.

Chloe is eager to get home and tell Mason about her new position, but she forgot about Mason Junior's football practice. She calls Sylve to get the latest at YI. Sylve tells her Riley has not been back since she quit. Riley has completely gone underground. Rumor around the company is Brett made her quit. Riley's brother Drew is highly upset and calls Brett a few choice names. Sylve says the names were so profane and distasteful that her mouth is pure compared to Drew's. And Sylve continues to vent her frustration over Channing's appointment.

With the news of Channing's appointing, Chloe hates to add fuel to the fire but delicately shares the good news with her.

Sylve snuffles and says, "I'm gonna miss my friend. This is bittersweet. I am happy. But you are leaving me. Who will I share my morning coffee and gossip with? Chloe, you know I like to demonstrate my weekend activities."

"Sylve, while you are talking about sin, I hope you are going to church."

Sylve was proud to say she went last week. While at church, she met the flavor of the month. Although she went with good intentions, a muscular and handsome man gravitated to her. Chloe has put their conversation on hold. Acer has a doctor appointment. She promises to allow Sylve to continue sounding off.

The Conversation

Whose report will they believe? We shall believe the report of the Lord.

Chloe and Acer arrive at Dr. Turray's office. While waiting to see the doctor, Acer squirms in the chair. Chloe knows Acer dreads being at the doctor's office.

She asks, "Are you feeling okay?" Acer, in turn, directs his question to his mom.

"Mom, is Mason Junior okay?"

Chloe is totally perplexed because she hasn't heard anything that would indicate otherwise. Chloe stares at Acer, trying to figure out why Mason Junior came up so suddenly. Chloe doesn't beat around the bush.

"Acer, why are you asking about Mason Junior?"

Acer begins to tell the conversation his dad had on the phone. He hesitates, squints, then turn and looks at Chloe to say, "Mom, promise me you won't get angry."

Chloe begins to get angry. Acer is talking so slowly. There are pauses between every other word. She doesn't want to frustrate her baby, but she is quickly becoming agitated.

"Acer, baby, tell me what's going on."

"Um, Mom, I think, I kinda heard Dad say, uh—"

Chloe wants to pull the words out of his mouth. She regains her composure.

"Acer, what—what did your dad say?"

"Dad said, um—that um—"

Chloe removes her bag off her lap. She rubs his back.

"Acer, baby, tell me. I promise I won't get angry."

Acer asked again, "You promise. Right, Mom?"

Chloe says, "Pinky swear. Now, baby, tell me."

"Dad said, um, Monica—"

Mrs. Astor, the doctor will see you all now. Chloe looks at Acer in disbelief.

"Son, we will continue this conversation in the car, And please try to remember."

The details are more important to Chloe than they are to Acer.

The nurse is attending to Acer, and Chloe is wondering what is happening.

She asks herself, *Is he trying to leave me for her? What games are Mason and Monica playing? They must not know Chloe Michelle Miller Astor.*

Chloe sees the nurse's lips moving but is not processing anything she is saying. The only words Chloe remembers hearing is Dr. Turray will be in shortly. As far as she is concerned, Acer is feeling better, and she needs to get to the bottom of Monica's next plot. Chloe wants to call Mason, but she remembers her promise to Acer. It doesn't stop her from thinking. Things are about to get heated.

It is almost a minute before Chloe realizes Dr. Turray is in the room. Dr. Turray has been Acer's pediatrician since birth, but Acer is terrified of doctors. He questions Acer about his school activities to ease the tension. Acer's answers are short and abrupt. Chloe rubs Acer's arm and tells him he doesn't have to be afraid.

Dr. Turray revisits the day of Acer's stomachache. He asks Acer to describe, as much as he can, what happened. Acer tells him what he had eaten. He continues on to say, "It started in the morning, but then it stopped. It would hurt then stop. When I was playing my game, it was hurting really bad. And it didn't stop."

Dr. Turray turns to Chloe who's still in the distance, confirms the x-rays didn't show anything. His diagnosis of a stomach virus is the same as Dr. Seagress. He reassures them that there isn't any reason for alarm, but they need blood work from Acer. Acer cringes when he hears blood. Chloe tries to comfort Acer and engage with Dr. Turray, but Mason, Monica, and Mason Junior have her preoccupied.

Getting blood work only took a few minutes, but to Chloe it was hours. Before they could get in the car, Chloe says "Acer, let's get back to our conversation."

Acer is playing with his game.

"Baby, that game will have to wait."

Acer wants her to promise she will not tell. Acer looks at his game and asks, "Mom, what is the last thing I said?"

Chloe can recall everything word for word, and Acer is trying to advance to the next level on his game.

"Baby, you said, 'Dad said Monica…'"

Acer remembers, "Oh yeah, Ms. Monica doesn't know he wants to leave."

"Who wanna leave?"

"Mom, you always correct Raysee and I when we say wanna. You asked me who wanna leave? Mom, that is not correct."

"Acer, you are pressing all the wrong buttons, and now is not the time. Forget my incorrect verb usage. I need to get to the bottom of this. Now please finish."

Acer continues, "Mason Junior doesn't want to play football, but his mom is pushing him and—"

Chloe is beyond frustrated at this point. She sternly asks, *"Acer and what?"*

He could hear the anger in his mom's voice.

"And he wants to live with us!"

Chloe is alarmed!

"Wait a minute! Mason who? Live where? What? Is that right?"

Chloe has to tell herself to calm down. She asked Acer who his dad was talking to. He wasn't sure, he thinks it was either Uncle Leon or Uncle CJ. When Chloe hears Acer repeat what his dad said, it eliminated Leon.

Acer adds, "Dad was getting frustrated and said, 'I should hang up the phone.' Then Dad kept saying it's all a mess and something else about Ms. Monica, but I don't remember."

Acer confirms what Chloe is thinking. Mason was talking to CJ.

"Baby, Mom has one last question for you. You don't have any idea what he said about Monica?"

"No, Mom, sorry. Dad did say that he couldn't tell you because you would throw him and Mason Junior out the house. You wouldn't do that, Mom, would you?"

Chloe explained, "There are some things I let slide. Then there are some things I don't play with. Your mom will not play games with her man and her money. I will leave it right there. Let's grab some dinner."

"Pizza please," says Acer.

"You got it. Now I have to call your dad."

Acer holds up his pinky and says, "Remember, Mom. Remember, don't tell."

All the while, Chloe is driving well pass the speed limit. She is eager to get home to find out why Mason is holding back critical information.

Mason doesn't know Chloe is making a beeline to get home. The last time he and Rick spoke, the conversation left an indelible print on him. He calls Rick and opens up about how all he can think about is their talk. To Rick, their chat was fruitless if Mason hasn't read his Bible. Rick points out "We run from God who can save us. We run to the devil who wants to destroy us."

Mason doesn't feel as empowered as he would like to be. Mason paces the floor for a minute and asks Rick, "Why do I entertain Monica? Why am I feeling unfulfilled?"

"Mason, what would you do if you told Raysen one hundred times to stop throwing rocks?"

"Man, after the second time, he would get punished."

Rick adds, "Well, Mason, pretend you are Raysen. The Holy Spirit has been trying to tell you to stop it for years. He will not take the rocks out of your hand. You have to lay them down. Now the enemy is bringing distractions because he knows you are not listening to the Holy Spirit."

Rick continues, "We exhibit behaviors for which there isn't an excuse. You cannot blame your mom or dad. The enjoyment of the act does not last, which is why you have to repeat it in your mind. Once it's in your mind, your actions will follow."

Mason knows in his heart Rick is absolutely right. He cannot not expound any further because Acer and Chloe are back from the doctor.

Chloe walks in the living room, looking exasperated. She greets Mason with a lackadaisical "Hello, Mason. Dr. Turray said it's a stomach virus."

Mason excitedly turns to Acer.

"Ace Man, Dad told you that you were going to be just fine. You're Dad's big boy. Now I want two for two. Chloe, did RAWLY offer you the job? Chloe?"

Mason is puzzled as to why Chloe is despondent.

He asks, "Chloe, you did say Acer had a virus, right. Is something else wrong?"

Mason stares at Chloe, and there's a scream from upstairs.

"Mom! Dad! It's Acer. His stomach again."

Mason, in disbelief, looks at Chloe.

"Chloe, y'all just left the doctor."

Before he could say anything else, Chloe is upstairs.

"Acer, baby, where is it hurting?"

"The same spot."

"Mom, why does Acer's stomach keep hurting?"

"I really don't know, Raysen."

"Chloe, maybe it's the pizza."

"I ate it and nothing happened to me. Let's get him to the hospital. Mason, your phone is ringing on the island. See if that's your parents."

"Hello, Monica, I can't talk. We have to take Acer to the hospital."

Before hanging up the phone, Monica tells him to keep her informed of how he's doing. When Chloe heard Mason call Monica's name, she wanted to scream. But Acer is more important.

She pauses for a second to say, "Mason, you didn't even have to entertain that foolishness."

"Chloe, please, not now."

Acer is pleading with his dad to stay home. He promises him it will stop like last time. Regretfully, Mason shakes his head no.

Mason tells Chloe, "Let's get Acer in the car, and we can call our parents while I drive. Chloe, I know we are dealing with Acer, but what else is going on?"

Chloe looks over the seat, stares at Mason, and turns her attention to Acer. While rubbing his entire body, Chloe sings his favorite sleep time song. Mason doesn't know why she is perturbed.

When they pull up, Chloe decides to bring Acer in herself. She tells the receptionist they were here not long ago, and her baby needs to see a doctor. Calmly she tells the texting receptionist, "Nothing has changed with insurance. And, ma'am, it would be in your best interest to just get me a doctor."

Chloe knows if that receptionist would have been uncooperative, she would be arrested. All of her frustration would unleash at that moment. Fortunately, the receptionist is cooperative.

The nurse takes Acer in the back. Mason is walking up when she tells Chloe they could wait in the family area. Acer turns around to Chloe.

"Mom, do I have to?"

"Yes, Acer. Baby, we have to find out why this happened again. We'll be right here, baby, when you get back," she replies.

"Hey, Ace Man, you'll be okay."

"Thanks, Raysen."

Chloe keeps saying, "I thought it was a virus. What else could be wrong with my baby?"

"Baby, don't start thinking the worse," says Mason.

Chloe turns around to see who Mason could have possibly been referencing because she is not his baby. She is one second from exploding on Mason, then her parents walk up. Mason doesn't realize what jeopardy he is in. "Mr. and Mrs. Miller, thanks for coming."

"Mason, you don't have to thank us. That's our grandson.

"Hey, Raysen, baby, come sit by Nana," says Catherine.

When Mason's parents arrive, Lilly sits quietly. Carter asks Mason how he is doing. Mason expresses deep concern for Acer. While Mason and Carter discuss Acer, Monica walks up behind Mason.

"Hello, darling. How's Acer?" she boldly asks.

"Monica? What are you doing here?"

Monica, with a smirk on her face, says, "Baby, I came to… Mason, Acer is our son's brother."

"Monica, you didn't need to come here. Monica, please leave," he says hastily.

Chloe hurries to Mason as fast as she could and tells him "you better send her home now, and I mean now."

Mason tells Chloe he will. Monica gets closer to Mason to say "I will leave, but text me with an update."

Lilly chastises her son, "Mason, stop it. Why did you ask her to leave? Son, she's probably concerned. After all, Acer and Mason Junior are brothers."

"Mom," a frustrated Mason says, "Acer is not her son. And I will leave it at that."

Chloe knows she is at her limit. She grabs Mason by the arm.

"Can I talk to you? Your ex walks in here pretending to show concern. Our son is back there again. We don't know what is wrong. If Monica returns, Acer won't be the only one back there. Monica will need a hospital bed. Mason Astor, I will not allow your ex-bed companion any place in our life. You slept with her. Now you fix it, and fix it now!"

"It is bad enough the devil is attacking Acer. I will not allow distractions, and I will not open the door for the enemy to come in. As far as your mom is concerned, this is not her fight. I respect her, but she better stay out of this."

"Chloe, she's probably just concerned."

"Really, Mason? She can keep her concerned self at home. One more wrong move from your mom or Monica, and you will be paying alimony and child support. You slept with that slut, so put her under your feet where she belongs."

Carter could hear Chloe. And after decades of living with Lilly, more than anyone he understands, he shakes his head, "Son, your wife is right."

"Dad, I didn't ask her to come."

"I'm sure you didn't, but you should have told her to leave immediately."

Lilly walks to them when she sees them talking.

"Carter, leave him alone."

"No, Lilly. This mess has to get resolved."

"No, Lilly! Carter, I know you are not speaking to me in that tone."

"Lilly, go sit down, please. Son, I have to agree with Chloe, you left the door open when she told you to text her. Mason, I know the both of you have a son together. You must have boundaries, or otherwise you will end up like…never mind. Acer is for you and

Chloe. Monica doesn't know her place. You have to be firm. If it doesn't come from you, you have invited trouble. Let me tell you, the devil never plays fair. He will take you farther than you plan to go and keep you longer than you plan to stay. You are the head of your family. Take control, son."

Lilly attempts to advocate for Monica, but the doctor returns.

"Mr. and Mrs. Astor, I looked at Acer's blood work, and I took a different test. I'm concerned with one area. There appears to be extra white blood cells in his digestive tract. I know Dr. Turray is his pediatrician. I want to refer him to a gastroenterologist for extensive testing. I will give him another prescription for pain. He will need to see a specialist by the end of the week."

"Dr. Seagress, we had an appointment with Dr. Turray today. They took blood from him also. Doctor, how serious is this?"

"Mrs. Astor, let's wait until we can get results from all the tests. The white blood cells can be a number of things, including an infection. He will be in room 6. You can go there now. The nurse is preparing the discharge orders."

"Mason, I can't lose our baby."

"Chloe, we won't lose him. Let's stay hopeful."

"Mason, do you really recognize the devil in all of this? You are looking at things on the surface, but they are deeper. How can you justify Monica coming here? You can't."

Mason promises to fix this situation. Chloe detects how she is in his system in the worse way. He has to purge her out.

"If you chose to lay with her and get fleas, that's your choice. But make sure you are man enough for the consequences. Only a weak man will violate his marital covenant for ten minutes to a woman with fake hair, fake boobs, and a fake ——."

"Chloe, Chloe, that's enough."

"I, Chloe Michelle Miller Astor, have everything natural. I'm so confident. I don't have to run for the light switch. I hope for your soul and the future of our boys that you put the devil where he belongs."

"Chloe, I am not in love with Monica. I love my wife. I love my children. Right now, our son needs to see a specialist. I am focused on us."

Chloe is beyond exhausted after leaving the hospital. She is undecided if she wanted to continue talking to Mason. She reclines in her favorite chair and prays for guidance. Ever since she was a little girl, her dad is her pillar of strength. This time isn't any different. She turns to her rock. Although she calls to say thank you, she needs to hear his voice.

Keith detects in her voice that something is wrong. He doesn't want to pry. He would rather she opens up of her own accord. He discusses trivial things, but Chloe is basically silent. After a few minutes of listening to him, she courageously discusses her suspicions of Mason's infidelity. Although she isn't sure, the signs are slightly apparent. Keith is highly displeased. His baby girl's happiness is of the utmost importance to him. He figures Mason's handling of the hospital situation has Chloe sad.

Keith and Catherine discussed the matter on their way home from the hospital. They did not appreciate when Monica showed up. Monica should not have been there. She uses her son to gain more access to Mason.

Keith wants to talk with Mason, but Chloe prefers not. The apparent stress has him very concerned about her. Today's ordeal took such a toll that Chloe forgets to sign the job's policy. Although she has a several hours to do so, the job isn't on her mind.

Keith questions the authenticity of Mason's behaviors. Chloe questions the validity of Monica's child. Keith defends Mason in the aspect of the boy being his. He thinks Mason Junior looks like Mason and Carter. Chloe has asked him a thousand times to take a blood test. Mason doesn't think a blood test is necessary because he knew what happened that night. This really bothers Chloe, and she hopes her brother doesn't find out.

Ray checks on her constantly. If he knew this situation has gotten to this point, he would be angry with Mason. On the day of their wedding, he made Chloe a promise.

"Sis, if Mason ever, I mean ever, starts tripping, I can promise you two things: when I shoot, I don't miss! I don't make no noise!" To eliminate confusion, Chloe loves her brother but wants to keep him at bay.

Keith usually talks with Ray on a daily basis. It had been a couple of days since they last spoke. Ray swings by the house when he wants a home-cooked meal. Ray faithfully helps his dad out in the yard. Keith always jokes how the cleanup could get done faster. But every ten minutes, Ray's phone beeps. Ray chooses not to marry. His philosophy is texting is cheaper than marrying because all he has to pay for is a data plan.

Despite Ray's single preference, Keith knows he is a good son. Ray dated Aris for almost two years. The relationship ended because Ray wanted it to revolve around him. Keith believes there is still a flame between him and Aris.

"Chloe, women are like gardens. You have to till them, tend to them, talk to them, protect them, and they'll grow. Once they grow, they take you up with them. I tell Ray these women who give it up after a meal and a movie are not worth his time. They look at his house and car and don't care about his heart and soul. They are not after him. They are after things and the security of things. They figure he's a good catch so they jump in his bed quickly. His lifestyle has played out. Because they give it, you don't have to take it."

"What is his answer to that, Dad?"

"At first, he used to say, 'Dad, a man got needs.' Aris wants to wait until she is married, and he doesn't have time to wait. Now he is beginning to realize which woman has the real value. He will have to break those strongholds."

"When he slept with ten women, he slept with the men they slept with and so on. I told Ray those ungodly spirits can transfer."

Ray's strong defense is how he wears protection.

Keith says, "Son, there isn't a prophylactic strong enough to stop the devil from coming in."

Chloe knows her brother cannot make excuses. She prays that God would bless Ray with the woman that he desires for him to have. She doesn't want her brother in the same situation as her. She is contemplating whether she made the right choice.

The Twist

One on one, you say, I say, we say but the last word is mine.

Chloe decides to take a long drive away from the awkwardness. Serenity, streams, and passing miles of creeks were a great antidote. She passes the lake where many of their childhood years were spent. Reflecting on the good times, she realizes what's really important in life. It's being a family, loving, laughing, and of course, jumping in the lake. This was their absolute favorite pastime.

On her way back, she remembers Acer has another prescription. Inside the pharmacy, she reads several magazine's hot topics while she waits. A bold voice over her left shoulder says, "Well hello, Chloe Miller." In an instant, she knows who it is. Before turning around, she thinks about the lake, her family, and how she doesn't like the way she looks in jailhouse orange. So, in a surprisingly calm voice, the words spill, "It's Mrs. Astor, Monica. And what do you want?"

"How's my stepson?"

"My son is just fine. And since you probably followed me here because I don't see you asking for medicine, let me give you some godly woman advice: I put the devil and all his flunkies under my red bottoms. So leave my family alone. If you ever show up at the hospital again, I promise on everything I love, you will need a room. My husband made a mistake when he slept with you, but that was before me. It was a costly mistake. His interest and only interest are Mason Junior."

"Chloe, you are insecure. You are scared. Your man will leave you!"

"Leave me? No, hon, I'm very secure. You are bitter because you have to pay for what I get for free."

"Chloe, I ain't bitter. Your husband is five seconds from my bedroom."

"And, Monica, you are two seconds from an asylum."

"Chloe Miller, when Mason and I were together, we made Mason Junior in one night. Ah how long did it take you to get pregnant? Talk now, Ms. Thing."

"Don't push me, Monica. I am giving you good advice. It's best you take it and run. When Mason and I shared our vow, we made a covenant with God. You wouldn't understand this because you are of your father, the devil. Monica, your prayers will ricochet, tread with caution. It is a dangerous prayer when you want God to bless you with somebody's else spouse. You are all over social media saying you love to praise God. Maybe you have a little god. You cannot praise my heavenly Father, plan sex, and pray to have my husband. You are twisted. And another thing, remember these words. For starters, you don't have a man now. Secondly, you couldn't keep Mason when you had him. And lastly, Mason doesn't even want you now. So that means you have three strikes—game over, chick. And by the way, this is a drugstore. Don't let your chase be in vain. Go get your medicine. It's on isle 5. Is that fish I'm smelling?

"Since you refuse to move, allow me to give you a final word before I leave. If all you have to offer a man is your body, you are a low profiting prostitute, and that makes you worthless. It is women like you that make young boys think they can have every girl they see because they saw their mom rotate men every week. You are teaching your son with your actions, not with your mouth. When he grows up and becomes a man and every other month it's a different woman, don't get angry. He got it from his mother. You planted that sinful seed."

The pharmacist tech yells, "Medicine for Acer Astor is ready."

Chloe points to Monica. "You were spared one more time."

The Tithe

Chloe learns a tithe is 10 percent of the gross. Anything less than a tithe is a tip.

Chloe finally confirms a start date with RAWLY. Her new team members are eager to find out what new and fresh ideas she will bring to the table. She understands the importance of this job and how it's an opportunity that seldom comes. At bare minimal, she is trying to put her life in perspective.

She observes Mason sitting at the computer in the other room. The drugstore drama is intentionally avoided. Very casually, she says, "I have an official start date." Mason stands up and kisses Chloe on her forehead. He hugs her with all his might. His expressions pierce her heart.

"Chloe, I want you to know that I am proud of you. You are my best love. I wouldn't want life without you."

"Really, Mason?"

"Yes, Chloe. I say let's go and celebrate."

"Is this Mason Astor I am talking to?"

"Yes, it is. You deserve this and so much more."

She maximizes this opportunity to address the tithe. "Mason, while you are behaving like a godly man, can we discuss our church contributions? This job is a blessing. God deserves more of our time and money. I was telling you this the other day. I keep sensing God is trying to get our attention. He blesses us so much, and we are living our lives like we don't need him. And that's not right."

Mason perceives going to church and giving in the offering are the same as tithing. Sunday service feels like a routine to Chloe, one that entails just going through the motions. Chloe discretely wants to pull 10 percent from their income, but she is steadfast against hidden agendas.

Mason's defensive stance keeps him questioning Chloe.

"What are you talking about? We go to church, and we give in the offering."

"Mason, we tip God but don't give our 10 percent like we should. When you, Rick, Jeff, and Alfonzo were hanging out in the strip club, y'all pasted mortgage money on those girls and didn't cringe. All they gave the rat pack was sticky fingers and imagination. Now you want to tip God a few dollars, leave church early to get to the football game, and sit in your $400 seat."

"Chloe, let me understand what you are saying. Who's in the kitchen?"

"It's me, Dad, Raysen."

"Bring Dad a sheet of paper."

"For what? Why do these children always ask for what?"

"Now back to you with your projected salary and mine. You are telling me, we will give the church about $36,000, give or take a few hundred a year."

Mason gasps when he realizes the amount. Ten percent in bold numbers are all over his paper.

"If you are thinking about 10 percent, we will have to move to a smaller house, and your high-end shopping is over. By the way, go to the paint store."

"What are you painting, Mason?"

"I will be painting the bottom of your shoes because, Mrs. Astor, your red bottom days will come to an end."

Chloe is determined to make spending adjustments if necessary. The inclinations in her spirit are right. Mason is being extreme to think moving is mandatory. The bottom line is, he doesn't want to give up those expensive boy toys and season tickets. Chloe already perceives they would save more money. But convincing him is a task. She wants Mason to promise that he will at least think about it. Chloe wonders if she will ever get a definitive answer as Mason leaves her suspended.

Chloe's phone is silenced while she discusses tithing with Mason. There are several missed calls from Sylve. When Chloe tries to call her back, Sylve's phone goes to voice mail. Mason's negative assumption has Sylve laid up with man number 101. Chloe and Sylve have been friends for a long time. Sylve disclosed some childhood pains that only Chloe was privy to know.

When Mason mentions sleeping around accusation, Chloe defends her friend's reputation. But he isn't convinced. Sylve gave up being promiscuous long time ago. Many times, she confesses to the temptation. She is trying to find her way. Sylve had it rough and overcame a lot of childhood trauma. Now she has her career, she makes good money, and she is faithful to her church.

Out of all Mason's friends, the only decent one is Rick. Jeff and Alfonzo still think and act like they are twenty-one years old. They are out there, bad and buck wild. Alfonzo is dating Patricia and Kelsie at the same time. Both women work at Chloe's job. He has the audacity to tell them Chloe can verify he is a nice guy. She ought to tell Patricia to ask Kelsie if he is a nice guy.

Chloe compares Sylve's church attendance to Jeff's and Alfonzo's. She goes on a regular basis. Mason's friends show up at Easter and New Year's like they are doing God a favor. She prays that they don't wait until they are in their seventies, eighties, or on a deathbed to get saved.

She didn't see any progress being made when Mason politely left the room. While discussing Sylve and YI, she has to contact Mr. Yale about her new position at RAWLY.

Chloe is apprehensive due to the fact that Mr. Yale will try to oppose her resignation. They developed a good relationship through the years. She leads in sales and is highly respected amongst her peers.

Mr. Yale desperately wants to keep her. In addition to his only daughter leaving the family-owned business, Chloe's resignation is another disappointment. Mr. Yale offers more money but to no avail. Chloe's decision to leave is final. However, she leaves him with recommendation of promoting other employees, specifically Sylve, and perhaps implementing bonuses. Sylve's bias attitude toward Channing diminishes after discovering Chloe advocates for her a promotion.

The next move for Chloe is to work with a sense of purpose instead of merely having a job. She knows working and having a job are two clearly distinctive terms. Going to a job often comes with compulsion and running to the clock at the end of the day, whereby working involves creativity and positive vibes. Basically, it's being where God would have her to be. She trusts RAWLY is the designated destination.

This moment in time makes Chloe grasp the importance of a perspective that channels eternal rewards rather than fulfilling worldly desires. Mason fully understands Chloe's purpose to leave YI. Even if he isn't understanding the tithing issue, at least he agrees

Chloe's path of life is purposeful. He is about to address it further, but his dad calls. There is an arousal of concern in his voice.

"Dad, are you okay? Is Mom okay?"

"Son, I got to get this off my chest. I cannot hold it any longer. For the last few months, your mom has been very uneasy. She snaps at everything I say."

"Dad, isn't that normal for Mom? She always snaps."

"Yes. But this time, it's worst. She is uptight and defensive. The defensiveness is noticed by a few ladies at the church. Elizabeth called me the other day because Lilly's phone was going to voice mail. When your mom returned, she told me she was with Elizabeth."

"Did you ask her about it?"

"Ask your mom? The answers are always evasive. You can't ask her anything without an argument. I thought perhaps—maybe—she isn't feeling well and asked her if she wanted to see a doctor. She told me, 'A doctor? For what? Are you sick, Carter? Because I'm not'"

"She makes these mysterious trips at least once a week. CJ asks if is she's having an 'old person affair.' I had to ask CJ what is an 'old person affair.' 'It's an affair old people have, Dad.' I don't know why I listen to CJ. I should have known that boy is going to say something bizarre."

"First of all, I told him we are not old. Secondly, no, your mom is not having an 'old person affair' as he so eloquently put it. Mason, then he asked me if my wife is a cougar."

"Dad, that's CJ. He will say stuff we all think."

"Mason, what is a cougar?"

"Well, Dad, a cougar is an older woman who sleeps with a younger man."

"I know my wife. She isn't a cougar or a cat. I thought perhaps she is hiding a sickness. I called your grandma and tried to be discreet, which I knew was impossible. She came straight out and asked what is going on with Lilly. I told her nothing. She said, 'Carter, she is my child. When she gets home, tell her I am praying for her. She might snap at you but tell her anyway and don't back down.' Maybe you can talk to her. Son, I don't know where to turn. I'm drained. It is hard. I love your mother through it all. These last few years have been more than I could take. I'm embarrassed how I am handling these matters. Mason, I cannot tell this to CJ. And Leon is hardly ever around, which I can't blame him. Son, I've been drinking. No one knows. And Lilly is so detached. She can't even notice. I did some things that I am not proud of. It has to end. I don't have the energy or strength to continue fighting for Lilly's love. If she doesn't get better, well, unfortunately…"

"Dad! What are you saying? I mean, I know Mom is a handful but ——."

"Son, she is more than a handful. She has become totally unlovable. Lilly is all about Lilly. When was the last time you heard laughter in our house?"

"I—I really don't know."

"Well, that's my point."

"Dad, I am sorry for what you have been going through. Why you didn't tell me this before?"

"Mason, you have your own problems. I became complacent and settled. I slack in many areas, mainly my church involvement. I should have been a better example of a Christian father. I'm not making excuses, but I am weary, enough of my situation."

Carter no longer wants to dwell on his problems. He asks about Acer, but Mason is processing his parents' marital issues. Carter's dilemma leaves him estranged. The upheaval of Lilly's cantankerous behavior has a domino effect.

For the very first time, as Carter details the dysfunction, Mason detects similarities in himself from his mom. He realizes that he and his dad are well-acquainted with stress, the processing of conflicting thoughts. They are pulled in two directions. It's a basic struggle to do the right thing when the wrong thing keeps vying for control. Before it's too late, they will have to decide who wins.

The Never

***

Do we hold on because we cannot let go? Do we hold on because it is best for us? Do we hold on because we are selfish?

Mason Junior, against his heart's desire coupled with trying to please his mom, decides to play football. Coach Brunson is surpassingly pleased with his skillset and performance on the field to the point that he is chosen to start. He has met a few friends, but his utmost wish hasn't come to pass. He still feels downtrodden. He wonders if his dad thought about his question. He doesn't regard his mom and her boyfriends as family. His maternal grandparents and uncles love him, but he wants to live with his dad.

He wants the setup and stability his brothers enjoy. When he is there, they play games with each other, ride their bikes, shoot a few hoops, and he is jealous. He has to go home to meet the new, and not going to be around for long, stepdad. Mason labels Monica's boyfriends as hoodlums who drink, play loud music, and smoke. Some of them are professional and career-driven men who cannot commit because they have a family.

Nevertheless, Mason Junior doesn't like any of them. His dad suspects abuse, and he is hiding it to protect his mother. None of Monica's boyfriends have harmed him in any way. They are only there for a good time with Monica. There isn't any interest in her son. If there happens to be a slight display of care for him, they have a motive. She has never received a proposal from any of the guys. It reflects what she has willingly become to them. To the single man, she's just an appetizer. To the married man, she's only dessert. Despite her ratchet behaviors, Mason Junior still loves her. Mason cannot understand what is pulling him away from her.

Mason knows Monica will go ballistic and think he put this idea in his head. Mason is absolutely certain that Monica will not allow their son to live in the house with Chloe. He will try to reason with Monica despite it being a challenge. He is trying to figure out a good way to address this issue. While he is contemplating, Monica dials him.

He greets her cheerfully. She is ecstatic. She thinks he has finally come to his senses and realizes who he needs in his life. Deep within, she prays he is about to say I am leaving Chloe. Their conversations aren't always about their son, so she is hopeful. His denial the past few months really meant yes. She has been trying to make him see it her way. Chloe makes his life miserable. His place is with her.

Monica's foolish self-persuasion is ignored. Mason's tone changes, and she associates it with detriment of some kind. She begins thinking of trouble at school, injury at practice, or anything. There is not any easy way for him to tell her.

"Monica, our son wants to live with me."

Monica is wondering if she is hearing correctly. She is looking around in disbelief.

Did he say what I thought he said? Our son wants to live with him. There is a minute of silence. Mason continues to call her name. "Monica. Monica."

"Mason, you must think I'm crazy. *Never*! No way! It will never happen. You are trying to take my baby from me. Who put you up to this? I know it's Chloe. I can see her name all over this plot. He will never be under the same roof with her. Never, Mason. And I mean never. Before I allow him to live with y'all, hell will freeze over. Chloe wants him there so you wouldn't have to help me. She is so selfish. It won't happen, Mason. You need to move out and come live with us. Your son needs you here."

"Monica, you need to put an end to your fantasy. I will never leave Chloe. I chose not to marry you. This is about our son. Stop it please."

"You wanna take my son from me and tell me stop it. You really want me, and I know it."

Monica promises Mason on everything she owns, it'll never happen. Mason Junior is all she has in this world, and he will not take him. He is a weak man for allowing Chloe to take their son.

Mason knows this is not Chloe's idea, but Monica is in such a rage he cannot reason with her. Monica thinks he is trying to protect Chloe. Monica didn't even ask if it was their son's idea. Her madness toward Chloe is nonstop.

"It's her idea, and I know it. I know how Ms. Thing thinks. Bye, Mason. I gotta go."

Chloe Miller will not take my son away from me. I let her slide at the pharmacy. But now this round is mine. She will never take my son away from me. She is lucky to get Mason. And what she doesn't realize is he is just minutes away from my bed. The nerve of Chloe to pull this stunt. Every time I think about it, I get angrier. If I don't deal with Chloe now, she will think her scheme worked.

"Hello, Chloe Miller. You know who this is. That's right. I got your cell phone number. I guess you're wondering how I got it. I will tell you. I got it when your man was sleeping in my bed. His phone was in his pants, and his pants were on the floor. Now you figure the rest out. But anyway, my reason for calling is to let you know that it will never happen. You will not take my son from me. If you think for one second I will let you take my son, you are highly mistaken. You don't want him. You feel threatened by me when Mason comes over here. You are mad because Mason is joyfully giving me money every month, and our son is in private school. You want to put that money on your feet or buy another ugly expensive purse. It will never happen, Chloe Miller."

"Monica, what are you talking about?"

"Don't play games with me, wicked witch. You know exactly what I'm talking about."

"Mason told me about your plot to take my baby away from me. It's not my fault you can't make another baby. But you will not take my son."

"Monica, you are a foolish woman being used and abused. Men rotate out of your life because you are easy. I can guarantee you, I am not trying to take your child. Don't call my cell again with your wild insinuations. As for Mason's pants being on your floor, that's your unlimited, untamed fantasy. You need tape for that mouth of yours and super glue for the other parts. And, lunatic, I know you remember the pharmacy, so don't push me. Goodbye."

The click from the phone infuriates Monica. Chloe recognizes how the battle is raging in intensity. She recalls, if *one can put a thousand to flight, two can put more.* Sylve isn't prepared for this yet. She has to go old school and get some help. She petitions Grandma Lera to pray for their family. She details Monica's lies and insinuations. Grandma Lera agrees to pray. She had given Chloe some direct instructions, which included reading the Bible. Chloe has not followed through. Grandma Lera knows this is the tool she needs to win this spiritual battle. She is a firm believer that troubles should never be wasted. But Chloe hasn't learned what God is teaching her.

"You need God's word to fight the unseen enemy. I'll back you up, but you got to speak it yourself," Grandma Lera says.

She wants to know if Mason was joining them in prayer.

When Grandma Lera discovers Mason didn't tell Chloe about the living arrangement, she is disappointed. As Chloe hears the garage door opens, she hangs up before Grandma Lera can tell her to calm down. She wants to say everything will be all right, but Chloe was gone.

Chloe approaches Mason the moment he enters the house.

"Mason, can I talk to you?"

"Is it about tithing?"

"No, I want to talk about Mason Junior or better yet Monica. How is it I am the last to know about these residential plans in my house? Do you really think I want to entertain Monica when my baby had to see a specialist?"

He sighs and sits at the island in the kitchen. He swirls and shakes his head.

"Chloe, I wanted to discuss them with you."

"When, after you discuss it with Monica? You should have brought this to me first Mason. When you go to her then come to me, you create division in our home, and you are functioning out of order. An "out of order" sign in the Astor's house means you aren't receiving any service, and you won't be giving any service. Read between the lines. I am your wife, not a playmate of convenience."

"Monica is the mother of Mason Junior, and that is her only five minutes of fame. She calls accusing me of plotting against her."

Mason continues to express deep remorse. This should not have escalated without Chloe knowing. He admits to his wrong doing, and she has every reason to be upset. It's easy to view a situation from one side. But when you are in another position, things look a whole lot differently. Mason's tunnel vision is a direct link to his selfishness. He fully comprehends Chloe's frustration, and he asks for her forgiveness.

This episode brought back memories to their college days. Mason had commitment issues while they were in college. The breakup happened as a result. Chloe refuses to give the devil leeway into their marriage, regardless of who or what he orchestrated. Their union is hampered by distractions of destructive forces. Chloe's foresight is an advantage, while Mason's hindsight refrains their progress.

Monica has too much unrestricted access in his life and their marriage. They spend more time arguing about her when they should be praying for God's purpose. Mason's few minutes with Monica become more regretful with each passing day. If only he could have seen how the enemy orchestrated this setup for his demise, he would have stayed home that night.

Chloe and Mason believe it is useless to fight Monica on this matter. Chloe is about to start her new job, and she needs her mind cleared. She can't afford to mess up. This promotion is a critical part of her destiny. They are being attacked by the devil with Acer's stomach, Monica's evilness, and strife in their marriage.

In addition, Mason forgets to add his mom to the list of attack. Something is going on with Lilly, and his dad doesn't know what it is. He has also been thinking about their previous conversation on tithing. He is ready to commit giving 5 percent to the church. Although 5 percent is half, his goal is the entire ten and more.

The Coffee

We can't keep doing this over and over. Something's got to give. Or better yet, somebody's got to give it up.

The morning starts off better than the day before. Dr. Mallory, Acer's gastroenterologist, calls with tests results. Dr. Mallory confirms it's a stomach virus. The good news of negative test results ripples through Chloe. She feels her family is heading in the right direction.

When she shares the good news with Mason, he replies, "Wow! The man upstairs got us through." His cliché isn't sufficient to Chloe. She wants him to call God's name. She wants a clear perspective on him rather than a cliché. He deserves their thanksgiving and praise.

The results could have easily been a dreaded disease, which a parent never wants to hear. It is a common thought that children bury their parents. Chloe counts her blessings of not being at the cemetery. It's never God's plan to kill anyone's baby. God has grace for mothers whose child is living or has transitioned living. It is his grace and unconditional love that levels the playing field, and that makes her equivalent with all mothers.

Grandma Lera is a testimony. Her broken heart has healed. Since he did it for her, he can do it for others. Chloe longs for Mason to acknowledge his grace that is visible in their lives.

Chloe is still rejoicing over Acer's test results. This news paves the way for her creative juices to flow for her first day on the job.

Mason grabs her by the waist.

"Baby, you are so beautiful. RAWLY is getting the best. I am privy to know this firsthand. Your first day will be fantastic. To celebrate, I have something for you. I purchased it for your office. It's a family picture we took last summer on vacation. The store cropped it, and I found the perfect frame. Let this be a constant reminder of how much your family loves you. If ever a day becomes topsy-turvy, look at this picture and know we are behind you 100 percent. I know it hasn't been easy, but things will get better. You are an awesome woman, Chloe. Whether you are wearing a fancy designer dress or jeans, baseball cap and a tee, you are spectacular, irresistible, and irreplaceable."

Chloe gets teary as Mason affectionately holds her. She is supported by three great loves, and she is grateful. Her level of confidence is boosted right on time. She winks at Mason as she sprays her favorite perfume.

"Mason Astor, tonight Chloe will make it rain and thunder so seek shelter."

Before she leaves for work, Chloe reminds Mason to update his mom with Acer's good news.

"Hey, Mom, where are you?"

"Mason, why does everyone keep asking me where I am? I am home."

Lilly is very defensive. Mason is thrilled to share the good news about Acer's tests results. He doesn't the get reaction he hoped for. She is blah and hurries to end the call. He manages to add the news of Chloe's new job. To his surprise, she says that Monica told her the other day.

This seems a bit suspicious to him. How could Monica have known? He doesn't want to push the issue with his mom. This day will not start off arguing about Monica. After all, his baby boy is well, and his darling wife is at RAWLY.

"Good Morning, Triss. I'm reporting for duty. I am ready to begin my season with RAWLY."

While walking down the hall, Chloe has a chance to meet a few people. Darlene meets her in the hall to provide the figures from last quarter. She is given the names of the employees that requires her supervision.

The partners are pleased with their decision to have her on board. Triss has the responsibility of making sure everything is in place. There is one minor issue that needs rectifying. They have to change the monitor in the office. In the meantime, Chloe roams the building. She decides to grab a quick breakfast.

Chloe relishes how this is a good move. The atmosphere at RAWLY is peaceful and conducive to productivity. As she stares around the building, she envisions promotion, and it puts a smile on her face.

"Good Morning, Mrs. Astor. That smile on your face is a bright spot in the café. I guess you are officially in the building. Congratulations. Would you allow me to pay for your breakfast before I leave? It wouldn't be a problem. I placed a to-go order a minute ago."

"Jonathan, thanks for the offer, but I'm good. You must have special privileges to leave work so early?"

"Business is business no matter where it's at. A man got to do what a man got to do. I'll see you around."

Chloe considers Jonathan the devil in a tailored suit. She wonders why is he so persistent. Although he smells good, looks good, and have the prettiest eyes, this would be a trap, and she is not stepping into it. However, he might be a good catch for Sylve.

As Chloe returns to her office, her phone beeps with a text from Lilly. She reads, "Have a great first day, Lilly." Chloe is baffled. While staring, she is confused as to why Lilly sent this. Is she dying?

Lilly texted Chloe while sitting in the park. Her date beckons for her. She struts over, and he kindly hands her a drink. He gives compliment after compliment. Lilly blushes and engulfs them all. He transforms her entire inner being with his words. The missing pieces of her life are coming together. This is overdue, and it fills decades of empty spaces.

Lilly is rejuvenated, but Carter's suspicion causes inward guilt. His accusations and questions are burdensome. He believes she is sick. Lilly is sick. She is lovesick. She strongly considers ending these rendezvous.

If someone, especially Elizabeth, recognizes her, it will bring a domino effect of devastation on her family. Elizabeth will call CJ. CJ will call Carter after proving his theory was accurate. Carter will call Leon and Mason. Mason will call Chloe. Chloe will call Lera. Since Lera's motherly instincts are always precise, this is too risky for Lilly. Her family devotion is at stake, but she is not ready to disclose.

He doesn't pressure her. The ball is in her court. He is very contented just being in her presence. Their meetings usually last for hours, but today it ended early. He has a busy schedule. Nevertheless, he leaves her with more uplifting comments. His week goes better after he has laid his eyes on her. She has changed his life for the better. His only regret is they should have met years ago. The comments make Lilly feel youthful, energetic, and vivacious.

When Lilly returns home, Carter looks her straight in the eyes and walks away. It is a look she has never seen before. She found it strange that he didn't question her. Lilly has been so preoccupied she doesn't realize Carter has long drifted away emotionally.

When he married Lilly, all his love and energy seemed inexhaustible. He provided unlimited affection and attention. Now through the years, Carter is depleted, and Lilly's selfish love didn't refill him. She continues to go back to that same well for water. Now it's dried up. She didn't foresee the impact and collateral damage on neither Carter nor Mason.

Mason's young adulthood could have been threaded differently had Lilly laid aside her one-sided view of life. Mason knows Chloe is a wonderful wife and mother, but he doesn't know how to love her. He said "I do" thirteen years ago, and he would say "I do" for the next fifty years. The *I do* and his actions are contradicting. Chloe is the love of his life. He is grateful that she didn't give up on her man. But he understands that he can't push her because she too is a work in progress.

Now whenever Monica calls, he declines it or ignores it. Monica notices that he isn't entertaining her calls. She has resorted to texting. Her last message notifies him of Mason Junior's scrimmage game tomorrow. Mason wants Chloe and the boys to accompany him at the game, but the boys had promised to help Ray clean Keith's shed.

With Chloe by his side, his underlying purpose is a united front. There are too many games being played. He wants to leave the past in the past. If he shows up to the game without Chloe, Monica would sense she has leverage. A man alone is isolation. And for Monica, that leaves open prey.

Mason contacts his best friend to say thank you. Rick gave him some undeniable truths. The heart-to-heart conversations were long overdue. It didn't feel good to Mason, but it was good for him. He credits him for saving his marriage. Being caught up in Monica's drama was bringing him down. His confidence in his flesh was monopolizing. The prayers of the righteous rescued him from the enemy's snares. What used to tempt him cannot tempt him anymore.

While others are praying for him, he will have to pray for himself. The devil studies him. He is familiar with his likes and dislikes, strengths and weaknesses. He will not tempt him with cake if he likes candy. He won't stop calling, but he doesn't have to answer.

Rick inspires him to be a godly example to his boys so they will mirror Christ to their children. Mason and Chloe have good insurance. But if all they can leave them is money, then they have left them empty.

Mason is beginning to notice some areas that were lacking. He is functioning on low levels that fed the wrong nature. He is a saved man behaving like an unsaved man. He thought being a man is centered around his manhood. He has made a commitment to attend Brotherhood Connection.

Rick's prayers are not in vain. He refuses to allow the enemy to gain strongholds in his friend's life. Rick holds the value of their friendship dear to his heart. Mason is proud to call him a friend and a brother. Their conversations are pleasing in the sight of the Lord. Raysen could not have a better godfather than Frederick Arthur Tillis III. Now they have to bring in Jeff and Alfonzo because hell is too hot, and eternity is too long.

"Rick, Chloe and I want to take you and Giselle out for dinner one day soon. Man, you deserve the best burger in town."

"Mason, I will laugh all the way to the steakhouse restaurant so bring cash and a card."

The Blood

The blood has never lost its power. It sets us all free. It cannot lie.

While walking to their stadium seats, Chloe cautions Mason that Monica didn't have any more strikes left. He rubs her back, ensuring her there will be no drama.

"Hey, Brenda," says Mason.

"Hi, Mason. Hi, Chloe. Glad y'all came. I was going to wait until the regular season starts, but my sister dragged me out here. I hadn't planned to sweat this early."

"I agree, Brenda. What did we miss? There was an accident, and we were in traffic," says Mason.

"It is the end of the first quarter. We're leading by three points."

As Chloe and Mason prepare to sit, Chloe spots Monica coming their way. She alerts him, but Mason doesn't hear. He is finagling with his stadium seat cushion and drops his phone. When he lifts his head, Monica is standing in front of him.

"Hello, Mason, darling."

"Monica."

"Mason, I was going to invite you to sit with me over there, but I'll leave you alone with your ugly duckling."

"Monica, Chloe is my wife, and you will not disrespect her. My wife and I will sit right here together. Now go to your section."

"Baby, thank you." Chloe chuckles and says. "I replaced my flats with tennis shoes just in case."

Mason ensures her again, she is covered. He prayed before they got there. She is deeply moved by his comment. She promises to demonstrate the power of a praying wife when they get home.

"Chloe, forget about Monica. Let's enjoy the game."

The fans are cheering for Prep-Con as Mason Junior runs with the ball. Mason is excited to see him in the game. He motivates him on every play.

"Run, son. We need a touchdown. Don't let him tackle you. Run. Run. Good move."

As the food vendor yells "Popcorn, cotton candy, hot dogs, sodas," Chloe reminisces.

She taps Mason.

"I remember your games. I sat on the fifty-yard line for every game. Your best game ever was played on the second Saturday in

October against our main rival. You scored two touchdowns and ran over one hundred yards."

He was amazed that she remembered. Their relationship had ended months prior.

"Those were some good days, but we have better days ahead," he says.

Mason continues to yell, "Come on, Panthers. Let's win this game. Run, son, run. Run. You got it. Run. Swerve to the right. Keep running. Look out, Mason Junior. *Ouch!* Chloe, that big boy hit him hard. Get up, son. *Mason Junior, Mason Junior! Masonnn Junior!* Oh God, something is wrong. He can't get up. Come on, Chloe."

Monica runs to the center of the field but is stopped. From a few yards away, she is pleading with her son to get up. Within minutes, blood is coming out his mouth. Monica is screaming to the top of her lungs. The EMT is pushing her back, but she is frantic.

"Ma'am, I really need you to step back. Let's get him on the gurney."

Monica touches him while he's on the gurney, leaving a blood stain on her jeans.

"Mrs. Astor, he is probably dehydrated," says coach.

Monica shakes her head in doubt.

"Dehydrated and bleeding. Coach Brunson, it has to be something else," she says.

Chloe hears Mrs. Astor, but Coach Brunson is not directing his conversation to her. Monica uses Astor on her son's school record for her last name. Chloe delays addressing it with Mason. As Mason Junior is strapped on the gurney, all teammates, except Foster, take a knee. Foster is tearing as he stands next to Mason.

"Mr. Mason, what happened?"

"Foster, I really don't know."

The EMTs report a fourteen-year-old male unconscious with possible internal bleeding en route to Lakelain's Hospital. The fans stand with faces of fear, terror, and dread as Mason Junior is rolled away. Brenda wipes her eyes and pats Mason on his back. Mason thanks her with a slight nod. Chloe delegates to update them on Mason Junior's condition.

Mason's tone of voice is barely above a whisper as he notifies his parents. What happened out there is rehearsed repeatedly in his mind. He pleads to God for mercy. A funeral comes to mind quickly. He casts it down, but guilt replaces it. Guilty thoughts of living arrangements and schooling are buffering.

Mason felt relieved when Acer's report was good—now this. he doesn't know what to make of it. Over in his head, he is saying what could have caused him to start bleeding. He thinks back to when he had been complaining, saying it's too hot. Perhaps this could have been avoided if he'd only listen to him.

"Chloe, I feel like I have failed him as a father. I couldn't protect him. All he wanted was to come live with us."

"Mason, don't allow the enemy to put negative thoughts in your mind. You didn't cause this. We have to pray. God healed Acer, and he can do the same for Mason Junior."

Upon arriving at the hospital, Mason replays thoughts of dread while pacing the floor. This could be the end for him, and he hasn't lived.

Dr. Hildcraft, the attending physician, walks in the waiting area, searching for Mason Junior's parents. He demonstrates with a model heart their son's condition. Mason Junior has a heart defect that went undetected. The heat and rigorous sport aggravated it, which caused him to pass out. The bleeding is a result of trauma to the chest.

"There is a fifty-fifty chance of survival. He has a few strikes against him. He lost a lot of blood, and he has a rare type. Unfortunately, we are nearly depleted at this moment. If Mason Junior survives surgery, his football career is over. This type of rare disease will restrict his life forever," says Dr. Hildcraft.

Dr. Hildcraft is reluctant. Mason senses there is more.

"What else, Dr. Hildcraft?"

"There is a possibility he won't make it past his eighteenth birthday. It's less than 5 percent chance he can live a normal life. Some have beaten the odds. I pray your son will be one of them."

A crushed, devastated, silent Monica touches her son's blood stain on her jeans. She rubs it over and over. She walks over to donate blood. The nurse tries to make small chat, but Monica is not responding. Chloe's heart aches for Monica. As unruly and evil as Monica is, she would not wish this on any mother. The pain and brokenness leaves Monica distraught. After giving blood, she aimlessly walks over to the chapel. Monica drops on the last pew. She cannot stop the tears from flowing.

Chloe and Mason stare at her through the glass windows.

Choe takes the initiative. She asks, "Mason, may I talk to you? I want both of us to donate blood. Your son lost a lot of blood, and our blood is needed, yours especially."

"Chloe are you sure?"

"Yes, I am 100 percent sure. I want us to do all we can to save his life."

"Chloe, thank you, baby. Thank you so much."

While they are discussing to donate blood, Mason's parents arrive.

Mason briefs them with a grim doctor's report. He stands eye to eye with his dad, repeating the events on the football field with emphasis of Mason Junior's nonstop bleeding. Carter is able to understand most of what he is saying. A few of Mason's words are mumbled. The detriment has Lilly despondent as she peeks around for Monica. Mason suspects she is looking for her so he points to the chapel. Mason becomes startled when Dr. Hildcraft returns.

Dr. Hildcraft explains the hospital is very, very low on blood. Mason Junior's blood type is *O*. He can give to anyone, but he can only receive from specific types. In the medical profession, he is known as a universal donor. While the staff is grateful for Monica's donation, her type is *A*.

Mason feels supported by Chloe in her endeavor to donate blood. Mason has severe anemia, but he will donate regardless.

Chloe sits next to Carter while Mason donates. They discuss anything but the present situation. In between topics, Carter plays with his cell phone. He has not engaged with Lilly since arriving at the hospital. Chloe is aware of the distancing. Carter validates her thoughts.

"I pray Mason becomes a better man than me."

She doesn't want to ask but rather ponders on what could be happening. She is startled when she sees the doctor. Monica walks out the chapel as she notices the doctor also.

"Dr. Hildcraft, is my husband okay?"

"Yes, ma'am."

"Is my son okay?" Monica asks.

"We are trying to stabilize him, but we desperately need blood. I am sorry and a bit confused. Um, is there perhaps another family member or someone closely related who we can test? This is a very serious matter. The problem is we cannot use Mr. Astor's blood."

Chloe approaches the doctor.

"Is it because of the anemia?"

"No, it's not Mrs. Astor," says Dr. Hildcraft.

"Then what is it? Tell me, Dr. Hildcraft."

"Perhaps you all can discuss this amongst yourselves, but he needs blood."

"Wait a minute! Dr. Hildcraft, what are you saying my husband just gave blood?"

"Ma'am, your husband cannot be the father!"

Monica screams, "You are lying, that's impossible! He has to match."

Chloe turns to Monica in disbelief and disarray.

"Monica, Monica, that child is fighting for his life. Is Mason the father or not? Is he? Monica, is Mason the father?"

"Chloe, I don't have to answer to you."

"My husband is on that table risking his life for a child that is not his own. Mason has severe anemia. All these years, you lied and deceived him. You are the lowest."

Carter tries to calm Chloe. She is at her limit with Monica.

"Monica, you are poison to this family."

Chloe envisions how something could have gone wrong, and her boys would have been without their father. When Mason discovers Monica's sinister plan, he will be devastated.

Mason walks out from the back, and all eyes are on him. He stands confused.

"What's going on? Did something happen to Mason Junior? Why is everyone quiet?"

Chloe breaks the silence. Delicately as possible, she unfolds the dilemma.

"Baby, listen, I'm sorry. You are not a match."

"Chloe, what are you talking about? I just gave blood. Do they need more?"

Mason is hearing but is not comprehending anything. His interpretation is that more blood is needed. He didn't understand his blood is not a match. The next few seconds are silent.

"My blood doesn't match. My blood *does not match! My blood! My blood!*"

With rage and resentfulness in his eyes, he braces up to Monica. Carter immediately pulls him back.

"Mason, don't hit her!"

"I won't hit her, Dad. I will kill her. You tramp. You liar. You lied to me all these years."

"Mason, move out of my face."

"My son, I'm sorry. Somebody's son is fighting for his life, and there isn't enough blood. Who is the father? Who? Or do you even know?"

"Mason, of course, I know."

"Who is he? Who the hell is he, Monica?"

"I don't have to answer to you. Mason, I did not force you in my bed. You were a grown man. You knew exactly what you were doing. You knocked on my door. You took off your clothes. You forgot? If you didn't want to be with me, you would not have answered my calls. All my calls weren't about Mason Junior, and you knew it. Yes, you told me to stop multiple times, but you never resisted me. You may have been in bed with Chloe, but your soul was in my bed."

Monica continues, "Chloe lays next to a shell of a man, the rest of you was with me. I bet Chloe doesn't know you were half a second from sleeping with me. Yes, I lied. I know he isn't yours. You could have gotten a blood test. What stopped you? You are not angry because Mason Junior isn't your son. You are angry because you got played. You feel slighted in the presence of your family, and your pride is hurt. Mason, the man who is untouchable, the man who thinks he has it all together—he's Mr. I got the answer for everyone else. Now he doesn't know what to do or say. The game you played on all those women came back and hit you right in the face. Don't act like you are brand-new to this. The only difference is I got caught. It happens to the best of us."

"Monica, when I say you are the worst mistake a man can make, I mean it from my heart. I do not want to see you ever. When Mason Junior gets better, I will tell him the truth. It was his idea to come live with us, not Chloe. By the way, Mason Junior doesn't even like football. He hates his new school. You don't even know your own child."

"And Monica, by the way, this will be his last year at Prep-Con. I will have a relationship with him for as long as he wants it. But I know he will want to know the truth about his biological father, and I wouldn't blame him. Don't call me. Don't text me. We have nothing to say to each other. Your child support has ended. I hope you saved the money I gave you because you will not get another copper cent."

"Money—that's what's on your mind, money? Keep your money. I only started pursuing you after my relationship with Samson ended. For over a year, you've been in my house seeing me with little to nothing on. You took those mental images with you to bed, and I know it. Mason, I don't feel any sympathy for you. You left me pregnant, thinking the baby was yours and married Chloe, and that makes you the worse mistake a woman can make. I have spent the last few hours in that chapel praying for my son. As far as I am concerned, you and Chloe can go straight to hell. And Mason, you will not have to discuss anything with Mason Junior when he gets better we are moving. I already have things lined up for us."

The nurse informs them a blood bank was contacted, and they will deliver blood tonight. Mason Junior is being prepped for surgery. The doctor projects three to five hours without any complications.

"Mason, I don't want you coming back to the hospital. I am his mother, and I know what's best for my child. I'd rather Mason Junior hurt for a few months than to hurt for a lifetime. We don't need you anymore. As a matter of fact, I want all of you to leave. Mrs. Lilly, I will text you when surgery is over."

Chloe drives them home. The mood is somber. Mason is conflicted. Fourteen years of his life were spent in betrayal. If he had only listened to his wife and Rick, this could have been avoided. He failed to measure the extent of Monica's evilness. His pride took precedence. For once, Monica was right. He could have taken a blood test. The lies and games on other women have reaped on him. He begins to pray for his sons. He wants them to live godly lives starting now.

The next morning, Chloe finds Mason in the kitchen. He was ending a call with his mom. Mason Junior's surgery went well, but he still has a 5 percent chance of surviving past the age of eighteen.

The boys are aware Mason Junior is hospitalized, but Mason didn't go into details about what happened last night. Mason took a few days off from work. Brenda cleared his schedule when she called for the latest update.

When Lilly called to inform him on Mason Junior's surgery, she also requested a family meeting. She wants to meet with all of them, but she did not give any indication as to what it pertains. Mason didn't have the energy or stamina to ask. He thought perhaps CJ might have an idea.

Reluctantly, he calls CJ. CJ doesn't know the reason for the meeting. Leon won't be there because he has to work, and he doesn't have time for Lilly's drama. Both of them exchange guesses. CJ proposes Lilly is going over her will. He will get half because he was born first. Mason and Leon each will get 25 percent.

"CJ, Dad says your brains are only wired for work. You are an engineer. But aside from work, you can't function in society. Let's focus on our mom. You don't have any idea why she wants to meet with us?"

"No, I really don't. And, Mason, I am sorry to hear about your son. Monica is a cold broad to say the least. Mom mentioned how you are not allowed at the hospital. That has to be hard. But you will have to stay away. Women like that are very unpredictable."

"And another thing, Mason, do you realize how much money she took you for?"

"CJ, now is really not the time."

"Fourteen years. Mason. Fourteen years. Oh my gosh, you could have bought a boat, a car, anything—fourteen long years of unnecessary child support. L'il brother, I thought I taught you better. Whew, just think. Prophylactics cost less than fifteen bucks."

"Big brother CJ, abstinence is free. Now bye."

As Chloe enters the building, she doesn't know if she has sympathy for Mason or anger for Monica.

If only he would have listened to me. His male ego superseded good judgment. How could he have fallen for such a classic trap? That is one of the oldest tricks in the book. I guess when the enemy has you blind, you cannot grasp the truth. I know of two men at YI who found out years later they were supporting children that weren't theirs.

Mason should have recognized the game. The first tell-tale sign was Monica didn't put him on child support. It wasn't because she was kindhearted. She didn't want to raise suspicion, and he thought he was coming out ahead. The winner was Monica—years of attentions and thousands of dollars on someone else's son. Now she cut him out of his life permanently.

When a heart is wicked, wicked actions will manifest. He never thought it would happen to him. A few minutes cost a price he thought he would never pay. The enemy doesn't come to play, he wants to destroy. I will have to try and put all this aside so I can concentrate. It's too early for me to mess up. After all, I just started.

"Hello, Mrs. Astor."

"Jonathan, not today please."

"You looked distressed. Is everything okay?"

"You are nosy, Jonathan, aren't you?"

"Actually, I am not. I am sincerely concerned. Can I help in any way?"

"Do you have type *O* blood to give?"

"Oh wow, wish I did. That's a tall order, Chloe."

"Chloe, Chloe. Who told you my first name?"

"Oh, I asked around. Sorry if it's out of line. Mrs. Astor, I would like to apologize. We got off to a bad and inappropriate start. Can we be socially acceptable friends at least?"

"No. Now move."

The Rise

Lilly has struggled her entire life. The stress has caused a domino effect.

Lilly gathers her family together, but inwardly she is uneasy.

I am so very perplexed and confused as to why I am choosing this method. I must be getting old because this is definitely out of character for me. I will have to make this short and sweet to eliminate any lengthy questions, especially from CJ.

As they enter, she follows her script. She greets them and orders them to sit in the living room. She stands in the middle of the floor, thanking each one by name for coming. Mason is the last person she thanks. He sits on the end of the sofa. After thanking him, she reaches over and kisses him. Mason is stunned but doesn't say a word.

Lilly addresses her family in a generic way.

"I know y'all are wondering why you are here."

She delays giving them a reason but extends compassion to Mason. Then she apologizes to Chloe for abetting with Monica. She should have stayed in her place. Chloe whispers, "Is she dying?" in Mason's ear. After a few seconds, Chloe accepts her apology but is apprehensive.

"Family, as your mom and a woman, what I am about to say is difficult. Carter and I talked at length the other day. We agreed this is the best way to handle things," says Lilly.

"What is it, Mom? Will this affect my 50 percent?" asks CJ.

"CJ, what 50 percent? Please listen, son."

"My inheritance, Mom." Carter tells CJ to be quiet.

Lilly acknowledges her defiant and inconsiderate ways. She walks toward Carter, takes his hand, and shares with her family his devoted, uncompromised, and unconditional love to her. As she shares her sentiment, tears flow.

"He has been by my side through it all. I have a love that I don't deserve. When God blesses you with such a special person, you have to be very mindful of how you treat him. Carter, I took your love for granted, and you could have left a long time ago. You are a better man than I am woman. Carter, for your love, patience, and faithfulness, thank you," says Lilly.

Carter wipes her tears and rubs her back as she tries to talk.

"I am not ashamed to say I am a broken woman, and only God can put the pieces of my life back together."

While Lilly is talking, CJ is saying to himself, "Old people affair. I knew it."

Lilly continues, "Before I met your dad, I was in love with a man. His name is Nash. Back then, biracial couples were not accepted. His parents made it known they did not want him with a black woman. They sent him away because he was in love with me. Well this is hard family."

Lilly holds on to the mantle. Carter reaches Lilly some tissue.

Chloe sits upright, saying to herself, "I've heard this story before."

Lilly continues, "As I was saying, Nash and I dated. And I got pregnant. I was ashamed. My parents sacrificed for Elizabeth and I. I disappointed them with my decisions. My life was not heading in the right direction."

"When Nash's mom found out about the baby, she threatened to take the baby if the baby was white."

CJ comments, "Mama, you had a—"

Lilly tries to continue, "CJ, not now. As I was saying, I got pregnant. My pregnancy jeopardized my family and those who love me. Dome, who was like a big brother to Elizabeth and me, was very protective of us. He was mad when I continued my relationship with Nash and begged me to end things because it was too jeopardous.

"One day, I went to talk things over with Dome, and he didn't want to listen. While trying to run after him, I fell. After falling, I was in constant pain and started hemorrhaging. I miscarried the baby. I went back to college and did not come home. I isolated myself as much as I could. I was in a depressive state. I knew the meaning of comfort food. I ate to ease my pain. One day in my dorm room, I began feeling very ill. Those same pains after the fall, reemerged. When I got to the hospital, the doctor told me I was in labor. When I miscarried, I didn't know I was pregnant with twins. I thought the weight gain was from eating. I didn't pay attention to my body. That night I gave birth to a baby boy.

"Nash's sister, Beth, was a nurse at the hospital. Mrs. Margaret found out about the baby. She took him from me, and there wasn't anything I could do about it. Many nights I cried myself to sleep. I held on to his blanket. It was the only bond that I had to him. I can still visualize his oddly shaped birth mark on his right thigh. That was the last image of my first-born son.

"Mrs. Margaret raised him as her own. I tried numerous times to sneak and see him, but my efforts were unsuccessful. I would ask around, and no one would tell me anything. Mr. Henry, Nash's dad, got wind of my snooping and threatened to hurt Lera and Joe if I continued to look for my son. I didn't want to put my parents' life in jeopardy anymore, so I stopped.

"When he became school age, Mrs. Margaret sent him to boarding school and changed his name on the school records. Years later at Mrs. Margaret's funeral, Mr. Henry was guilt-stricken. He told his Nash about the baby. Nash looked for him but couldn't find him. After boarding school, he moved abroad.

"Through years of investigating, Nash eventually found him. When he looked into his eyes, there was no doubt. Nash told him the truth. He became determined to find his biological mother. About one year ago, he moved here. He took a job downtown. He searched the county records to find me.

"Family, as the tears flow, I want you all to know this is the hardest thing I ever had to say. All these years of heartache and heartbreak, a secret was buried in my heart. One thing is for certain, truth will always rise.

"My son, whom I hadn't seen since his birth, found me. He called and asked would I meet with him. I agreed and wasn't sure how he would react. As I stared into the eyes of my firstborn son, a load lifted. I had a son out there and didn't know what to do. We have been meeting once a week, getting to know each other. It is hard to be a mom after all these years to a grown man."

"Does he call you mom?" asks CJ.

"No, CJ. We are on first name basis. I asked him to come this evening to meet his family. We can't turn back time, but we can move forward. He met your dad a few days ago. Now I want to introduce him to all of you."

"Jonathan, come out," says Lilly.

Chloe is alarmed and yells, "Oh my gosh, I can't believe it."

"Chloe what's the matter? Do you know him?" asks Mason.

"Yes, Mason. She knows me. I pursued her before I found out she is my sister-in-law. I tried to apologize. Mason, you have a zero-tolerance wife," says Jonathan.

"My life has been an interesting turn of events. I am blessed to have met our mom. Most of my life, I have been lied to and deceived. It caused me to become untrustworthy. Now my life has come full circle. My grandmother gave me everything except what I needed most, and that was the truth about my parents.

"CJ, I know you are concerned about your inheritance. I am the sole heir to my grandparent's estate. I guess it was their way of compensating for the many lies through the years.

"This is an adjustment for us all. Nevertheless, I am willing to try. I could only hope you want to do the same."

Mason says, "Welcome to the family. Chloe, baby, now he can buy you coffee. Jonathan, Chloe has a best friend she can introduce you to."

"Family, I would like to add one more comment. Chloe, as I said earlier, I'm sorry. My defense of Monica was personal. I didn't want another woman to be like I was—without her son. My reasons were selfish, and I magnified an uncomfortable situation. I functioned from pain instead of love. I am still not where I need to be, but I want to get better."

The Enemy

The thief comes to steal, kill, and destroy.

After dismissing Monica's lies and processing Lilly's son, Mason and Chloe were able to enjoy an intense, intimate night without interruptions. Chloe believes a fresh start of rekindling is in motion, but there is still troubling in her spirit. The next night, as she prepares for bed, she tosses restlessly and wants to wake Mason. She stares at him, realizing he is a man she doesn't know but thought she knew.

As darkness gives way to light, their bed is flooded with ungodly spirits. Chloe realizes she had been sleeping with the enemy. They were invited long before she knew Mason. The enemy didn't come to play, he came to stay. Their oneness is hindered by the enemies he slept with and never cut off. Under no circumstance, in any situation, sleeping with the enemy is ever beneficial.

Regardless of Mason's physiological strength, he could not reach Chloe where it mattered mostly. They needed oneness in spirit without any contributions from the flesh. Although the moments were deep and intense, he thought being physically out of an ex's bed was the solution. The soul ties infiltrated their home because they were still in his soul (emotions, intellect, and will).

Having to deal with the enemy that is not visible to the human eye was challenging. If the curtains were drawn, they could see the devil as the puppet master orchestrating their demise. He wants to devour and destroy God's children. Since the enemy is a spirit, the fight can't come from the flesh. It has to come from resurrection power.

The spirit that drove Mason to mistrust and feel unstained had decades and generations attached to it. His capacity to pain exceeded his capacity to love unconditionally. It charters a pathway to living unknowingly in dysfunction. It piloted his mother's thoughts and actions.

Lilly had a powerful spirit of rebellion, control, and arrogance, coupled with never-ending thirst for her first love. She could not let go of Nash. Her bitterness grew and lodged in all four quadrants of her heart. Lilly plugged her pain with deception and could only love Carter in fragments.

She thought it was masked, but Carter wasn't getting all of her. Wine and whiskey solidified his void and led him to solo acts in the bathroom to imagine and fantasize about what he needed but didn't get. Afterwards, he could crawl into bed and kiss Lilly good night, thinking he was unconditionally loved in his mind, even if it was just for those few minutes.

Although Lilly confessed about Jonathan, no one thought to pray that night while they were all together. More than finding her son, she needed to invite God into their family. It is the Astor's family's hidden curse that developed relationships without fulfillment. Chloe gave Mason all she had, but it never reached him because he did not know what he did not know.

Chloe decided in her heart, what was tolerated will no longer exist. At 3:00 a.m., she tosses and turns, restless. She meditates on worship service from the day before. The guest pastor from Texas preached on living life or living dead. His message came from Romans 8:6–7. She recalls him talking about being carnally minded and how it's like the living dead. She was the living dead. Thinking like the world and operating from the flesh does not bring spiritual blessings. She recalled Grandma Lera's advice and grabbed her phone. She read Romans 8:6–7.

As she pondered over her life, she found no trace of time for God. With tears flowing, she gets out of bed and drops to her knees. She opens her heart to God. She lifts her hands to heaven and surrenders fully to him.

She says, "God, this is Chloe. My life has been me, my husband, my children, my family, and my job. I put you in wherever and whenever I could fit you in. I am sorry. Forgive my heart. Forgive my actions. *Create in me a clean heart, and renew in me a right, true spirit.* My life is yours. The house, cars, job mean absolutely nothing without you.

"Pierce the darkness. We need your direction. Heal my husband from the pains of his past and deliver him. Heal our marriage. Deliver Monica. Heal Mason Junior. Love me, God, and let me love you. Cover us with the blood, and don't take your spirit away from me. In Jesus's name. Amen."

Mason rolls over and sees Chloe's face drenched from her tears. At first he doesn't know what to make of it. When Chloe gets off her knees, he holds her and doesn't want to let go. He whispers, "I saw you on your knees. It seemed like you were giving God all of you. I heard you call out my name. You even prayed for Monica. And all I could say is 'God, forgive me'. I spoke with Rick about changing my life, but I never asked God to forgive me. I need to know his will for me. I've done me a long time, and it has gotten me nowhere. I have to surrender to him. And the rest of my life is his. Most importantly, heal and deliver our family from the pains of the past."

She told Mason that's a good place to start. It could not have happened at a better time. In six more months, a new life will come in this world. Masie Lera Astor will live from the blessing and not the curse because her mom and dad were set free.

Whom the son sets free is free indeed.

Isn't God, our good and perfect Father who loves us despite our faults, secret sins, planned sins, bitterness, and _____ (you fill it in), able to deliver us if we only ask him?

The Life

◆◆◆◆◆

For to be carnally minded is death, but to be spiritually minded is life and peace. Because the carnal mind is enmity against God: for it is not subject to the law of God, neither indeed can be. (Romans 8:6–7 KJV)

Following after the Holy Spirit leads to life and peace, but following after the old nature leads to death; because the old sinful nature within us is against God. It never did obey God's laws, and it never will. (Romans 8:6–7 TLB)

I call heaven and earth to record this day against you that I have set before you life and death, blessing and cursing: therefore, choose life that both thou and thy seed may live. (Deuteronomy 30:19 KJV)

I call heaven and earth to witness against you that today I have set before you life or death, blessing or curse. Oh, that you would choose life, that you and your children might live! (Deuteronomy 30:19 TLB)

About the Author

Ellen is a born-again believer, thankful for the victory emanating from Jesus's death on the cross. It is his grace that underlines her life. This truth was instilled at a young age from her parents' spiritual and educational tutelage.

Ellen earned a bachelor's and master's degree. For the past twenty-eight years, her career has been immersed in therapy and manages virtual academics.

During her collegiate years, Ellen's research was published in Association of Research Directors proceedings. Spiritual guidance led to the writings of After the Benediction and the successive work, *Nite: Never Invite the Enemy*. Each novel confirms Ellen's belief in the power to overcome and accentuates her Southern roots. She continually raises the banner high as she passionately calls Louisiana home.

9 781638 742401